# THE
# JAMES DEAN
# STORY

# THE
# JAMES DEAN
# STORY

## A MYTH-SHATTERING BIOGRAPHY
## OF AN ICON

**Ronald Martinetti**

A Citadel Stars Book
Published by Carol Publishing Group

A Citadel Stars Book
Published by Carol Publishing Group
Citadel Stars is a registered trademark of Carol Communications,
Inc.

Editorial, sales and distribution, rights and permissions inquiries should
be addressed to Carol Publishing Group, 120 Enterprise Avenue,
Secaucus, N.J. 07094

In Canada: Canadian Manda Group, One Atlantic Avenue, Suite 105,
Toronto, Ontario, M6K 3E7

Carol Publishing Group books may be purchased in bulk at special
discounts for sales promotion, fund-raising, or educational purposes.
Special editions can be created to specifications. For details, contact
Special Sales Department, 120 Enterprise Avenue, Secaucus, N.J. 07094.

Manufactured in the United States of America
10  9  8  7  6  5  4  3  2  1


Martinetti, Ronald
    The James Dean story : a myth-shattering biography of an icon / by
Ronald Martinetti.
        p.   cm.
"A Citadel Stars book."
ISBN 0-8065-8004-6
1. Dean, James, 1931-1955.   Motion picture actors and
actresses—United States—Biography.   I. Title.
PN2287.D33M37   1995
791.43′028′092—dc20
    [B]                                                        94-25243
                                                                  CIP

*To the memory of Shari Levitt*
*and the glow of her rainbow*
*and for Thomas Whitney Rodd, Esq.*
*—teacher, martyr, saint—*
*this book is dedicated*
*with deepest affection*

*I would like to especially acknowledge the help of the late Rogers Brackett, without whose openness and cooperation this book could not have been written: and for Elia Kazan, who suggested the approach which I have tried to follow: "Just tell the truth."*

# Introduction

James Dean was little more than a boy when he died, killed at twenty-four on the highway near Paso Robles, California, on September 30, 1955, while on his way to a sports car meet. At the time of his death, Dean had completed three movies, *East of Eden*, *Rebel Without a Cause*, and *Giant*, only the first of which had been released.

Dean was already an actor of promise, and his death was front-page news. It was the Eisenhower era—a time of peace and prosperity—when young people were expected to respect their elders and obey the rules. But even during his short life, Dean was widely known as a nonconformist—a rebel who had taken Hollywood by storm and who did as he pleased.

For young people coming of age, Dean was someone they could easily identify with: an outsider, a loner—he was the antithesis of everything a well-behaved youth was supposed to be. His screen portrayals symbolized the rebelliousness of adolescence. In public he was often rude, even surly. A fan magazine quoted him as saying, "I wouldn't like me, if I had to be around me." He had been known to fight with directors and storm off the set. "Jimmy knew what young people were up against," an admirer once said. "He understood." Later, someone else referred to him as "the first student activist."

From the day of his death, it seemed that young people would not let Dean die. A special fan mail agency had to deal with the deluge of mail that poured into the studio. Many of the letters were addressed to the dead star.

A record, "His Name Was Dean," put out on a small label, sold twenty-five thousand copies in a single week. Mattson's, a Hollywood clothing shop, received hundreds of orders for red jackets identical to the one Dean had worn in *Rebel Without a Cause,* and Griffith Park, where scenes from the movie were shot, became almost overnight a tourist attraction. Admirers lined up inside the Observatory, hoping to sit in the same seat Dean had used in the film. "It's like Valentino," a reporter told Henry Ginsberg, the coproducer of *Giant,* Dean's last movie, referring to the craze that had swept the nation after the Italian actor's death in the 1920s. Ginsberg disagreed, "It's bigger than Valentino."

Some fans refused to believe that Dean was really dead. Walter Winchell printed in his column the rumor that Dean was disfigured but still alive. Other stories insisted that it had been a hitchhiker and not Dean who had been killed and that the actor was in hiding while learning to operate his artificial limbs or that he had been placed in a sanatorium.

Hollywood, of course, had always been a commercial enterprise: Dean's popularity was not lost on the moguls who had built the industry. Jack Warner admitted: "That kid Dean...gave us a lot of trouble, but it was worth it. He was surrounded with stars in *Giant,* but we believe he was twenty-five percent responsible for the success of the picture." Aided by studio press releases, fan magazines printed stories with titles like, "You Can Make Jimmy Dean Live Forever" and "The Boy Who Refuses to Die."

Not everyone, however, was enthusiastic about Dean. Herbert Mitgang, of the *New York Times,* dismissed him as "an honor graduate of the black leather jacket and motorcycle school of acting and living it up." And director Elia Kazan, Dean's mentor, claimed: "Every boy goes through a period when he's seventeen or so when he hates his father, hates authority, can't live within the rules...It's a classic case. Dean just never got out of it."

Dean's recklessness and commitment to having lived his life

to the fullest had its appeal as well. "All adolescents," wrote Martin Mayer in *Esquire*, "want to rope steers…and sculpt busts of famous novelists and drive a custom sports car and write poetry and be a great Hollywood star. Dean did it.…In a way, the kids feel he did it all for them." He was, moreover, the one hero who would never sell out. He would never have a chance to.

A few of Dean's close friends refused to take part in the hysteria—or cash in on the enterprise. Dennis Stock, a young photographer, remembers being invited to dinner by another photographer, Sanford Roth, after Dean's death. Roth had been the still photographer on *Giant* and had shot numerous poses of Jimmy both on and off the set. When Stock arrived, he assumed that he and the Roths would spend a quiet evening reminiscing about their gifted friend. But when he realized the Roths had invited a newspaper reporter who was doing a story on Dean, Stock got up and left. "It was a publicity setup," he recalled with disdain.

In a sense, however, Dean had almost invited the reaction that followed his death. "He was a boy with a wonderful sense of the theater," director George Stevens said. As a farmboy, in high school, Jimmy had been a show-off; in Hollywood, he cultivated his offbeat image with the press. After making *East of Eden*, Dean excused his obnoxious public behavior by telling an interviewer, "I can't divert into being a human being when I've been playing a hero, like Cal, who's essentially demonic." On another occasion, he explained: "A neurotic person has the necessity to express himself and my neuroticism manifests itself in the dramatic…" He was—cool; the perfect quote was always on his lips.

Humphrey Bogart, who also knew a thing or two about image making, once said: "Dean died at just the right time. He left behind a legend. If he had lived, he'd never have been able to live up to his publicity."

But Dean did not live and in death became transformed into a myth: Even today, visitors come from all over to visit his grave in Fairmount, Indiana, the small farming community where Dean grew up. In one recent year, there were over six thousand visitors, some from as far away as Argentina and Australia. Dean's handsome, brooding face adorns posters and T-shirts. A licensing company, run by lawyers, markets James Dean calendars, postcards, and ashtrays around the world.

Over the years, an impressive list of actors and performers have claimed to have been influenced by him: Bob Dylan, Al Pacino, Martin Sheen, Michael Parks, the late Jim Morrison, poet and lead singer for the Doors, who lived fast and died hard, just like one of his heroes, James Dean.

Dean's life has been the subject of novels, plays, even a song by the Beach Boys entitled, "A Young Man Is Gone." But not every writer has been adoring. In 1993, George Will, the respected conservative columnist, blamed Dean and his film personality for the youthful unrest that convulsed the country in the 1960s. Will wrote: "In *Rebel*, Dean played himself—a mumbling, arrested-development adolescent—to perfection. Feeling mightily sorry for himself as a victim (of insensitive parents), his character prefigured the whiny, alienated, no-body-understands-me pouting that the self-absorbed youth of the sixties considered a political stance."

But Dean was a many-sided figure; the sullen young man was only one facet of his personality. He was creative, intellectually curious, and ambitious, as well as manipulative and extremely selfish. Many actors who actually worked with him disliked him—and rued the experience. One actor who worked with Dean on TV recalled decades later that Jimmy had been vulgar, self-congratulatory, and rude. "His movements on stage were far removed from the carefully rehearsed-planned positions," the actor recalled. This created "havoc with the other actors' performances and for the director. The result was pandemonium for everyone except Mr. Dean and his sick ego." This comment is all too typical and an ironic epitaph for an actors' icon.

Moreover, not all of Dean's friends found him loyal. After

Jimmy had achieved success, a struggling young photographer to whom Dean had reason to be grateful asked him to go halves on a used camera. Dean refused. "I can get all the new equipment I want," he said callously. Alas, this was not the only friend Jimmy left behind after his rapid rise to fame.

In the years since Dean's death, there has been much speculation about his rumored bisexuality. In fact, women were strongly attracted to him, and he engaged in numerous affairs. At one point, in New York, he was simultaneously having affairs with a wealthy debutante and a beautiful high school girl.

A few Dean friends continue to deny his homosexuality, despite conclusive evidence to the contrary. After reading a draft of this manuscript, actor Martin Landau refused to be interviewed, saying: "This guy was not gay." Only one of Dean's homosexual relationships is dealt with in this book—and that in his early days in Hollywood and New York with a director named Rogers Brackett.

Brackett was a well-connected figure in Hollywood; the son of a Hollywood pioneer, he knew everyone from Marlene Dietrich to Henry Miller. He got Dean small parts in three Hollywood movies and later helped him land his first starring role on Broadway.

After Dean's death, Rogers regularly refused press interviews about him and turned down biographers' requests. His own attainments were considerable: a witty, cultivated man, he had directed stage plays and had written lyrics for a popular Alec Wilder song. Brackett had no desire to be regarded as an appendage to his famous protégé.

Toward the end of his own life, however, when he was stricken with cancer, Rogers granted me the only interviews he ever gave on Dean. He was tired of the "half-truths" that had been published and wanted "to set the record straight." This book draws on those interviews and the letters he wrote me; many of the items are published here for the first time, since Rogers requested that they be withheld until after his death.

As we approach the fortieth anniversary of Dean's death, however, neither his sexuality—nor the quirks in his personality—make much difference to his ever-growing legion of fans: Bikers and mall rats, poets and rockers revere him as much today as teenagers did a generation ago. To them, he is what he is: a rebel for all seasons.

Ultimately, it seems, as long as there are young people, so long as there are boundaries, Dean will live—and the legend will endure.

# THE
# JAMES DEAN
# STORY

JAMES BYRON DEAN was born in Marion, Indiana, on February 8, 1931. The delivery took place at home, in an apartment building known as the Green Gables, on East 4th Street in downtown Marion. At birth Dean weighed eight pounds, ten ounces. The doctor's bill was fifteen dollars.

James Dean's father, Winton, was a tall, thin dental technician who worked at the veteran's hospital in Marion. The son of Charles Dean, a Quaker farmer and local auctioneer whose forebears had come to Indiana from Kentucky in 1815, Winton was regarded as a taciturn individual. Even after his famous son's death, he was seldom interviewed. An acquaintance once described Winton as possessing "the characteristic Dean traits of softness, reticence, and a manner of speaking so slowly and hesitantly that you wanted to prod him with a stick."

James Dean's mother, Mildred Wilson, was the daughter of a Gas City, Indiana, factory worker. Her family were Methodists. A short woman, pretty but a bit on the plump side, she had black eyes as sharp and bright as a sparrow's. Around Grant County it was rumored that the Wilsons were part Indian; as proof, people pointed to Mildred's eyes. There the evidence ended, but even years later when her son became famous as an actor, someone who worked with him on Broadway dismissed his sometimes wild behavior with the excuse, "He was part Indian, you know." Legends often die hard.

Mildred Dean was a quiet and sensitive young woman.

Among her neighbors she was thought of as being somewhat distant, even a bit of a dreamer. "Mildred was never exactly sure what she wanted," a friend in Marion once recalled. "If she bought a new dress on Tuesday, nine times out of ten she'd return it to the store on Wednesday."

Even as a girl Mildred had been deeply interested in the arts, and after her marriage, music and books provided a welcome diversion from the tedium of small-town life. She played the piano well and was fond of poetry.

When her son was born she gave him the romantic-sounding middle name Byron, after her favorite poet, Lord Byron, the poor boy who became a dissolute lord and romantic legend.

When Dean was four, his father was offered a post as a permanent staff member at the Sawtelle Veteran's Administration Hospital in Los Angeles. After talking it over with his wife, Winton accepted the job. The family moved to a five-room apartment at 814-B Sixth Street in Santa Monica, and the following year Jimmy was enrolled in the Westwood public school system.

Even though the Deans were a young couple struggling to meet the expenses of their new household, Jimmy had all the toys he wanted and, if anything, seemed to be spoiled beyond his parents' means.

"He had a large anxiety to do many different things," his father later told a magazine writer. "He had to try everything, and he soon outgrew most of the toys we bought him. He always seemed to be getting ahead of himself."

At his mother's insistence, Jimmy was given violin lessons at a very early age. There were also tap dancing classes, and these pursuits, coupled with the fact that he was somewhat under-sized for his years, set him apart from other children. At school he had difficulty making friends; his classmates ridiculed his musical studies and teased him about his middle name. He had his share of boyhood fights. Looking back on his early childhood, Dean later chuckled: "I was anemic. I was a goddamn child prodigy."

Mildred Dean never felt comfortable in California. She missed her family in Indiana and felt isolated in her new surroundings. To a friend visiting from home she confided that she would like to return to the Midwest. "Everything's so artificial here," she complained. "I want my son to grow up where things are real and simple."

Although Mildred had been close to her son before, life in California drew them even nearer. She read books to him and devised games that they played by the hour. For one of their games she built a cardboard theater, and using paper dolls as actors, they took turns making up plays and stories. In her spare time, Mildred also took a beauty course, hoping to supplement the family income.

Then, in May of 1940, shortly before her thirtieth birthday, Mildred Dean developed severe chest pains and was hospitalized; her condition was soon diagnosed as cancer.

Winton Dean's mother came from Indiana to help out during the illness. Mildred's chances of recovery were not good, and should the worst occur, Grandmother Dean had come prepared with an offer to take young Jimmy back to Indiana to be raised by relatives. She was in California only seven weeks when Mildred died, on July 14, 1940.

Bereft, deep in doctor's bills from his wife's illness, Winton Dean agreed with his mother to let Jimmy return to Indiana with her. At the time, he spoke hopefully of sending for his son as soon as he got back on his feet. Eighteen months later, however, he was drafted into the Army, and whatever plans he may have had were permanently shattered.

Jimmy and his grandmother rode east on the same train that carried his mother's body home.

Many years later in Hollywood, Dean blurted out in a famous interview with broadcaster Wally Atkinson, "My mother died on me when I was nine years old. What did she expect, me to do it all by myself?" But to those who knew him best, the loss of his mother was a searing experience, one Jimmy never got over. His chronic insecurity, a need for attention, the searching for a love that always eluded him—all seemed to stem from that terrible and irreparable boyhood experience.

The relatives who welcomed young Jimmy into their home were the Winslows—Winton Dean's sister Ortense and her husband Marcus. Honest, hardworking, they lived on a farm just outside of Fairmount, a small town in central Indiana with a population of twenty-seven hundred.

At the time Jimmy came to live with the Winslows they had been married eighteen years and had a daughter, Joan, fourteen. But they had always wanted a son, too, and eagerly accepted Jimmy into their household. They even gave up their own room and moved across the hall because he liked their maple bedroom furniture.

The Winslow house still stands on the edge of a 178-acre parcel of land. A big white house built in 1904, it is situated on top of a small hill, and the land gently rolls down to the farmyard with its white barns and sheds. The farm has sheep, chickens, and pigs; there are some forty acres of oats and long rows of corn. The land here is fertile—the so-called black soil belt of Indiana—and the Winslow's farm yielded a comfortable, though modest, existence. "We're not rich, but we're not poor either," Grandma Dean said. "So long as I live, I'll always have a porch to sit on, a rocking chair to rock in, and a clock that strikes."

In a short time, as the Winslows had hoped, Jimmy began to fit into the routine of farm life. Life on the farm was busy. There was livestock to feed and corn to plant before the rains came and the hard midwestern winter set in. Young Jimmy was given his own chores to do: milking the cows and helping Marcus feed the livestock. It was not long, his cousin Joan recalled, before he was pestering everyone to teach him how to drive the Winslow tractor. Once he learned, he forgot about the tractor and wanted to raise chickens instead. This impetuousity was to remain characteristic his whole life.

In the summers there was swimming in the Winslow pond, fishing for carp, and family picnics. Aunt Ortense was always near, ready to comfort her nephew. When he cut his finger doing chores, it was Ortense who would tape it gently. One neighbor thought he "looked too fair for a boy," but his aunt glossed over the comment as nothing more than prattle. Like other farm boys, Jimmy joined the local 4-H Club. In the fall of 1946, he won a ribbon for a soil project he undertook.

To Uncle Marcus, Jimmy "was a boy, just like any other boy, always chasing some sort of ball...." When the large pond froze over, Jimmy learned to skate, and his uncle rigged up electric lights so that Dean and his friends could play hockey at night. On Sundays, the family attended Friends Back Creek Church. Afterward, friends and neighbors would meet at each other's homes for dinner. Before his death in 1976, Marcus said of his nephew: "He was raised decent, but they say he was ill-mannered and ill-bred.... I don't understand that." The boy he remembered used to tag around him opening gates so he wouldn't have to get off his tractor.

Nevertheless, Jimmy got into his fair share of mischief. Looking back on those days, he once said that he liked to "wrestle and kill cats and fight—things boys do behind barns," he added in candor. "He was always climbing trees and fences he wasn't supposed to climb and finding new ways of getting into trouble," remembers Helen Walters, a schoolmate. "Once he rigged up an elevator from the top of the barn and nearly broke his neck when the rope snapped. Another time he almost got drowned exploring a fenced-in pothole that was supposed to be bottomless. I guess he was kind of a show-off, but everybody liked him, especially the girls." Others who knew the actor as a child recalled traits he never outgrew: He was moody, unruly, unpredictable.

On one occasion, trying out a new stunt, Dean lost his four

front teeth and had to be fitted for bridgework. He had been swinging on a rope in the Winslow barn, trying to imitate a trapeze artist, and had fallen to the ground. Knowing it made a better story, Dean would sometimes later tell people he had lost his teeth in a motorcycle accident. He had a good imagination and never hesitated to put it to use.

Jimmy seemed to be a born mimic. At school, with a little prodding from his friends, he could quickly do imitations of various teachers; once, when Dean was in the middle of an impersonation of the school's principal, the man happened by and overheard him. Supposedly, he was so amused by the boy's talent that he failed to punish him. Perhaps this is true.

At family gatherings Jimmy would entertain everyone with his mimicry. His family encouraged his talents and liked to speculate that perhaps he took after his great-grandfather Dean, a well-known local auctioneer who was famous for his ability to entertain a crowd while disposing of his wares.

When Jimmy was ten, his aunt asked him to read for a medal at the Women's Christian Temperance Union (WCTU), an organization in which she was active.

Over the years, he won a number of silver and gold medals for his dramatic readings before the WCTU, and Aunt Ortense looked forward to the day when he would compete for the organization's highest award, the pearl bar. "The way they had things," Dean joked, "you could go to hell just for stepping on a grape." But to satisfy his aunt he took part in the readings.

On the night of the competition for the pearl bar, however, there was a track meet at school that Jimmy wanted to attend instead. His aunt insisted he read for the prize. Reluctantly, Jimmy went to the hall and, when his turn came, got up before the audience. He stood there several minutes, not saying a word, then walked off the stage, to the embarrassment of his aunt. Afterward, he said his mind had gone blank.

"I was sure then of what I had known all along," Ortense said. "You couldn't make James Dean do anything he didn't want to do."

For his thirteenth birthday, Jimmy's guardians bought him a Whizzer, a small motorized bike. With the help of his uncle, Dean learned to ride the machine and soon handled it so well that he outgrew it. He traded it for a small used motorcycle of Czech make. "Start an Indiana boy with a jackknife," his grandmother commented proudly, "and he'll end up swapping for a house and lot." By the time Jimmy began high school, he had his own full-size motorcycle that he raced on a local dirt track.

Marvin Carter's motorcycle shop became a favorite hangout of Jimmy's. Years later, Carter still remembered the sudden way Dean would come into his shop, slightly out of breath, and say, "There's something wrong with my cycle. Can you fix it now?"

If Carter told him no, Jimmy would ride away. "You'd think he was mad as the dickens," Carter added. "But five minutes later he would be back again, calmed down. 'When can you fix it?' he would ask."

To Jimmy, waiting was a terrible waste of time; nor was the ability to sit still ever counted among his virtues. When he wasn't pestering Carter with endless questions about whatever machine the mechanic was then working on, he would occupy himself entertaining the other boys who usually crowded the shop. One of them remembers that Dean liked to stand at an imaginary public address system, pretending to call out a race. "He'd get us all lined up," he recalls, "tell us what kind of weather it was, who got the jump, who crashed at the first turn, whose motorcycle was bursting into flames. Damned if he didn't make it sound so real, I had to look twice to make sure I wasn't really racing."

To the citizens of Fairmount, Dean soon became a familiar sight racing through town astride his machine. "He sounded like a rocket," a store proprietor said. "You could hear him coming three miles away." Dean delighted in doing daredevil feats such as racing while lying flat on the saddle. "If he'd only fallen once, things might have been different," his uncle later reflected. "Trouble is, he never got hurt and he never found anything he couldn't do well almost the first time he tried it. Just one fall off the bike and maybe he'd have been afraid of speed, but he was without fear."

Despite his seemingly outgoing personality, Dean appeared to have few friends, and none that he was close to. "Jimmy considered himself an outsider in town," observed Joe Hyams, a writer who knew him in Hollywood, "and people in Fairmount quickly regarded him as being different." Unlike most boys his age, commented Hyams, Jimmy "spoke his mind when he felt like it, and he liked to be left alone." Once Dean was expelled from school for fighting with another pupil, Dave Fox. The boy had laughed during a dramatic reading Dean was giving, and this led to a fight outside school. Dean apologized and was reinstated the next day.

In appearance, Jimmy was thin and on the wiry side; always small for his age, at his full height he stood only five feet eight inches—a fact that studio biographers would always do their best to improve upon. Extremely nearsighted, he was forced to wear thick glasses. "He was blind as a bat without them," an acquaintance said. "I don't think Jimmy ever took them off, not even when he went to bed."

Among his schoolmates, Dean bore the added stigma of being virtually an orphan. Although he had come to call Ortense "Mom," he was aware that, unlike others at school, he did not live with his real parents. Moreover, Dean's father rarely visited him, and the boy's sense of desertion grew. Throughout his life, he never won his father's approval. Friends who saw them together in later years had an uncomfortable feeling that the taciturn figure did not like his son. Whatever its root, there was simply this distance between them. Dean's great screen roles were to capture the poignancy of that separation.

When Jimmy was fourteen, the Winslows had a son of their own, Marcus Jr., and suddenly Jimmy was no longer the center of attention in the household. Ortense now had a baby to care for, and instead of spending all his spare time with Jimmy, Uncle Marcus began sharing it with both the boys.

To win acceptance, Dean turned to athletics. "I had to prove myself back there," he once said. He began a self-imposed regimen of workouts: running, lifting barbells, copying exercises from a physical fitness book he had bought. In the Winslow barn his uncle had set up a basket, and Dean spent hours alone practicing shooting and learning to dribble the ball.

His efforts paid off well: Freshman year at Fairmount High School he made both the basketball and track teams; by sophomore year he earned his letter in baseball as well, playing around the infield.

On the basketball court he became an outstanding player, making up for what he lacked in height with a quick, aggressive style. He broke at least a dozen pairs of glasses, his uncle claimed. Opposing teams soon singled him out as the man to stop.

Although Dean won the respect of his teammates, Coach Paul Weaver discovered the little guard required special handling. "He wasn't too coachable," Weaver said, a comment directors would echo in the future. "I had to be careful about changing his style of play, and I soon learned not to embarrass him in front of other boys."

In 1948 Dean received his first press notice, an item that appeared in the sports pages of the *Fairmount News*. It called the junior guard "an outstanding threat on the high school team," and mentioned he had "accumulated forty points in three games." Dean's senior year the Fairmount Quakers reached the finals in the sectional tourney, but, on February 26, 1949, lost to a tougher team from Marion, 40–34. In a losing cause, Dean scored fifteen points, a high for both teams. A quarter century later, Coach Weaver remembered: "Like most athletes, he suffered with his teammates the agony of defeat." But, the coach added, "As I recall, personal performance was extremely important, win or lose."

Having grown bored running the high hurdles on the track team, in his senior year Dean decided to take up pole vaulting. Mastering this new challenge excited him. "Track," he liked to say, "gave me the sense of discipline I needed." It has always been part of Dean folklore that in his very first meet as a vaulter he broke the existing record for Grant County. But Paul Weaver, who also coached the track team, remembers no such event. The existing record, the coach recalls, was then about eleven feet, and Jimmy's best effort was about ten feet six inches, "a good vault for a high school boy of that time and place." The coach later wrote in a letter: "Like many others, I remember Jim as a quiet, clean-cut young man, not much interested in *showing* his like or dislike for others. [emphasis in original]. I don't remember Jim as one who worked at cultivating friendships. His talk and mannerisms on screen appeared to be Jim Dean and not so much playing a part."

Outside of school Dean became friendly with a local Methodist pastor, the Reverend James A. DeWeerd. Like Dean, Reverend DeWeerd was something of an outsider in town. Originally from Cincinnati, DeWeerd was a former Army chaplain who had served in World War II. He had been with the infantry at Cassino and had suffered a severe shrapnel wound. For this, the army awarded him a Purple Heart as well as a Silver Star, for gallantry under fire.

Well educated, a man of many interests, DeWeerd prided himself on his cosmopolitan views. In music his taste ran to Tchaikovsky, and his conversation was often sprinkled with quotations from the works of writers he admired.

In Fairmount DeWeerd was treated respectfully, although there were some who didn't know quite what to make of this stocky preacher who read poetry and practiced an exotic form of self-discipline called yoga—it helped, the reverend explained, ease the pain of his war injuries.

To Dean, DeWeerd became almost a hero. In turn, De-Weerd sensed in the young boy an inquisitive mind. "The more you know how to do," the pastor told him, "and the more things you experience, the better off you will be."

Under DeWeerd's tutelage, Jimmy's horizons gradually began to broaden. DeWeerd loaned him books from his library and showed him movies he had taken on his travels. One evening he showed a film he had made of a bullfight in Mexico, and Dean was fascinated by it. For the rest of his life, bullfighting was to be one of his great passions and one of the few things in which he never lost interest.

From DeWeerd, Dean learned something about music, as well as the other arts. He even tried his hand at sculpture, and one afternoon brought a small clay figure to DeWeerd for his approval. The minister carefully studied the work, a four-inch statue of a boy sitting with his head lowered introspectively, his hands covering his face. "It's me," Dean stammered. "I call it *Self*."

To DeWeerd, though, Jimmy was more open than he was with others. He spoke to him about his mother and confessed the guilt he had felt because of her death. DeWeerd did his best to comfort him. "All of us are lonely and searching for answers," DeWeerd later said, "but because he was so sensitive, Jimmy was lonelier and searched harder."

When Dean was a senior in high school, DeWeerd taught him to drive a car and took him to Indianapolis to see the famous Memorial Day race, the 500. Dean was thrilled by what he saw and was swept up by the excitement of the crowd and the increasing drama of the afternoon as the race wore on. All the way back to Fairmount he talked of nothing except the race and Cannonball Baker, a driver he had briefly met.

It was an afternoon DeWeerd would remember grimly when, six years later, Dean perished on his way to just such an event, and DeWeerd was asked to conduct a memorial service for his young friend.

In school Dean's interests also began to expand beyond the athletic field. He joined the debating society and was elected president of the Thespians, the school drama club. He played the clarinet in the school band and liked to imitate Benny Goodman, whose records he collected. On one club trip he visited the grave of Buffalo Bill, the frontiersman and carnival performer who also became a legend.

"[Jimmy] had a bright mind but didn't always apply himself in high school," his aunt said. "He used to say, 'I'd rather not get good grades than be called a sissy.' But his last year in school he promised he'd make the honor role and he did." Dean received two A's and two B's, one of which was in math, a subject he disliked. Only a lone C in U.S. Government marred his report card.

School plays, though, were what interested Dean the most. Decked out in a papier-mâché costume, he played Frankenstein in a Halloween skit, *Goon With the Wind,* and appeared in a production of W. W. Jacob's *The Monkey's Paw.* In the fall of 1947, his junior year, he played the part of Otis Skinner in *Our Hearts Were Young and Gay.* "Whatever ability I may have (as an actor) crystallized back there in high school," Dean said later.

Senior year he tried out for the lead in the school production of the Kaufman and Hart comedy *You Can't Take It With You,* but lost the part to another student, Joe Eliot, who later went to work for a finance company in Marion. Jimmy had to settle for a smaller role, playing a mad Russian.

Students who worked on stage with Dean found him talented—and temperamental. Adeline Nall, who coached the school's drama club and also had Dean in her advanced speech class, remembers, "There were times when Jimmy and I were on the outs. We used to squabble when he was my student. We'd always get back together somehow. Once he offered me a cigarette in class just to be smart. I almost popped him. He was just that kind of maverick kid."

At the urging of Miss Nall, Dean decided to enter a contest held by the National Forensic League in March of his senior year. He chose as his selection Charles Dickens's "A Madman's Manuscript" (from *Pickwick Papers*) and stayed after school working with the teacher to polish his reading. The monologue was about "this real gone cat" Dean remembered fondly in the be-bop bohemian lingo he was to later develop.

At the state finals held in Peru, Indiana, Dean breezed through and was an easy winner over a student from Culver Military Academy. "I came on stage screaming and tearing at my clothes," Dean said. "Really woke those old judges up." One judge was impressed with the "eerie expression" in the actor's eyes. "They actually looked glassy and mad at times," he recalled. Dean won a small silver trophy for his efforts.

Accompanied by Miss Nall, the budding thespian then traveled to Longmont, Colorado, to compete in the finals.

Two years before a hitchhiker named Kerouac had passed through the town, on his own sojourn. "It was beautiful in Longmont," he was later to write.

A small, quiet town nestled high in the Rocky Mountains, Longmont opened its doors gladly to the contestants who poured in from around the country. Students and their faculty representatives boarded with local families, and the town arranged picnics and square dances to help entertain its young guests. For a solid week everyone had a ball; Dean's hosts even allowed him use of the family car.

Dean mingled easily with the others, meeting students from all over. He struck up a friendship with some girls from the South, and within no time was playfully mimicking their accents, to everyone's delight. He also met a young boy his own age from New York, Jim McCarthy, and the two became inseparable.

McCarthy regaled Dean with stories about New York, and Dean listened eagerly to his new friend's tales of crowded streets and night baseball games and a basketball team called the Globetrotters made up entirely of Negroes who were all wizards with the ball. "Three baseball teams in one town," Dean kept repeating. "Jeez."

Dean was away from home for the first time and enjoying himself, and Miss Nall now found him even harder to handle.

In its original presentation, Dean's reading ran twelve minutes, but Miss Nall wanted him to revamp it to run closer to the ten-minute mark the judges now asked for. Dean refused. "We'd go round and round," Miss Nall remembers. "He was a very strong-willed boy."

Dean also refused to wear a coat and tie like the other contestants, instead wanting to appear on stage in jeans and an open shirt. "I can't do the piece if I don't feel it," he said. "How the heck can I go crazy in a suit and tie? It wouldn't work."

Dean won his argument with the teacher, but as she had warned, he did not do well in the contest. The award went to a girl from Santa Rosa, California. Dean was not even among the finalists.

The budding actor was shaken by this setback. On the train back to Fairmount, recalled Miss Nall, who is now in her nineties, Dean just sulked, hardly saying a word. "He blamed me," she said, "and I blamed him."

Even years later, even after making *East of Eden*, Jimmy could not come to grips with the fact that he lost the contest, telling interviewers that after winning the state championship he had not gone on to Colorado. He never quite forgave Miss Nall, either. "That chick was a frustrated actress," he said.

Back in Fairmount, as graduation approached, Dean and his classmates laid plans for the future. Uncle Marcus had hoped that Jimmy might go on to college at his alma mater, Earlham, a small Quaker school in nearby Richmond, Indiana, and take up agriculture. Jimmy, however, told him he wanted to study acting. The Winslows had heard this before, but had regarded it as another phase their nephew was going through: In the past he had also spoken of becoming a painter or a lawyer, only to later announce that he had finally settled on medicine. Once he even confided to Miss Nall that he was thinking of entering the ministry. "I wasn't surprised," she said. "He would have made a powerful minister."

But after his return from Colorado, acting was all Dean

talked about. If he had tasted defeat in Longmont, he had heard the sound of applause, too. And it was a sound he liked.

When the Winslows realized he was firm in his intentions, for the present anyway, they decided it would probably be best if he went to school in California; there he could get better training and would be close to his father as well. Winton Dean agreed, writing that he would like Jim in school near him; about his son's plan to study acting he appeared less enthusiastic.

For Jimmy, graduation day, May 16, 1949, was a proud occasion. He graduated in the top half of his class (twentieth out of forty-seven), and was selected to read a prayer at the end of the graduation ceremonies. The school voted him a medal as best all-around athlete, and he was given a prize by the art department as outstanding student.

Within two weeks, he was packed and ready to leave for California. His diploma and awards were tucked away in the tattered brown suitcase his aunt had given him. He spent the early morning saying good-bye to some friends around town and made a quick last-minute check on his motorcycle, stored in the Winslow tool shed.

His aunt and uncle drove him to the Pennsylvania Railroad depot in Marion. It was early June, but the sun was uncomfortably hot in the Indiana sky. Jimmy seemed not to notice it, talking excitedly as they rode to the station.

He was eighteen, and he was on his way to California to be an actor.

**2**

IN CALIFORNIA Dean rejoined his father, and for a short time everything went well. Still living in Santa Monica, Winton Dean was now a supervisor at the Veterans Hospital, having returned to his job after his discharge from the army. He had remarried in 1945; his wife was a woman named Ethel Case, whom he had known before.

Winton was glad to have his son back home, but it soon became apparent that the years of separation had taken their toll. A gap had grown between them that father and son found impossible to bridge. Later, Winton said: "My Jim is a tough boy to understand." To make matters worse, Jimmy resented his stepmother, and Ethel Case, a proud, strong-willed woman, was quick to sense it.

Over dinner, Winton and his son quarreled frequently over Jimmy's plans for the future. To Winton, acting was "a waste of time." He urged his son to consider something practical, like becoming a physical education instructor, or studying law—a field in which he could utilize his talent for public speaking and, moreover, earn a good living. In fact, Jimmy himself went back and forth between his yen for acting or becoming an attorney. He later said that stories of Clarence Darrow and Earl Rogers, two legendary trial lawyers, had whetted his interest in criminal law.

Dean and his father also disagreed over which college Jimmy should attend in the fall. Jimmy had planned on UCLA, which had an excellent theater department—and a good basketball team, too. His father preferred Santa Monica City (now Junior) College, a two-year school, which was closer to home and where tuition was lower.

Things, however, were not all bleak. Jimmy had discovered the existence of a theater group nearby and was accepted into its ranks. The group was made up mostly of housewives and businessmen, amateur actors drawn together by their love of the theater. They met in the evenings, using whatever facilities they could obtain for their rehearsals.

Dean painted scenery and helped with the props. "I seem to be getting a very cheap theater education," he wrote exuberantly to his aunt and uncle in August. "The work I am doing is easy and advancement is unlimited as to talent...(but) we get very little pay if any. I am certainly impatient, but getting a foot in the door of the movie world is a long, tough job...." He went on to humorously characterize his newfound comrades in the theater as "the most catty, criticizing, narcissistic bunch of people you ever saw, always at each other's throats. But let an outsider try to interfere and they flock together like a bunch of long-lost buddies....What a life."

"I learn a lot from them," he added. "I've just got to be patient, I guess. They never made it until their twenties, thirties, and even forties."

For his efforts backstage, Jimmy was rewarded with a small walk-on role in a musical melodrama called *The Romance of Scarlet Gulch*. In the program he was listed as Byron James, which he then considered adopting permanently as a stage name. For all his feigned sophistication, Jimmy was still a naive young boy, struck by the glamour of the acting profession. At this time, Gregory Peck and Jennifer Jones were among his idols; Stanislavski and the Method meant nothing; the Actors Studio might as well have been on the moon.

Winton Dean got his wish and Jimmy enrolled in Santa Monica City College for the summer session that began on

June 20, 1949. He took a cross section of required liberal arts courses: English, geology, physics, and Spanish. As an elective, he signed up for a class in theater arts. During this time he lived with his family at their Sixth Street apartment, in a quiet, tree-lined neighborhood.

Santa Monica was a small school with an enrollment of sixteen hundred. It had been founded in 1929 and was then located in a temporary cluster of buildings on Seventh Street and Olympic Boulevard while awaiting completion of its new campus across town.

Jimmy found himself very much a big fish in a little pond. He announced for the school's FM radio station and during his first semester was elected to the college Honor Society. He even made the Santa Monica basketball team as a substitute guard. The college belonged to the Metropolitan Conference, playing such opponents as Ventura and Los Angeles City College. Dean got in about half the games. Sanger Crumpacker, the team's coach, remembers him as "a tolerable good guard" and "a leader who went for the ball."

He also found time for dating and went steady with a girl named Diane Hixon, a willowy blonde who was elected homecoming queen.

Dean rooted for the football team, the Corsairs, seldom missing a home game. When several students chartered a bus to San Diego to see the Corsairs play, Dean and Diane went along. Jimmy had too much to drink at the game and was ill on the ride back.

Since Dean did not have a car, he often double-dated with Larry Swindell, a classmate who owned a black Chevrolet coupé. They often took their dates to the Cave, a dark coffeehouse frequented by students, or drive out to the Point, a place where they could drink beer overlooking the ocean.

Swindell and Dean were both in the school jazz club, and some afternoons they would go down to Ray Avery's Record Roundup, then on La Cienega Boulevard. Dean liked Bessie Smith and Jelly Roll Morton and would pick out old 78s on the

Brunswick label. He bought records by Kid Ory, the New Orleans sidegate trombonist, and Frank Trumbauer, the saxophonist who played with the legendary Bix Beiderbecke in Chicago.

Swindell, who is now a book critic on a Fort Worth paper, recalls, "Dean fancied himself as sort of a Renaissance man. He was interested in everything and had the idea that he could do a lot of things well."

Once Dean and Swindell went to hear a lecture, "Is Progress Real?" given by Will Durant at the Santa Monica Auditorium. Durant concluded that indeed much progress had been made in this century. Dean was very impressed and later quoted Durant around campus.

Despite all these other activities, however, Dean still found time for his interest in drama. "He would study continually in all areas of dramatics," his teacher, Mrs. Jean N. Owen, recalls, "and was enormously self-educated, a self-starter, and very self-motivated." One project he tackled was a radio comedy that he worked on with a friend. They tried to sell it, but were unsuccessful.

Along with classmate Dick Mangan, Dean organized and acted in a May Day production of *She Was Only a Farmer's Daughter*. The show was put on at the Santa Monica Theater Guild. Mangan later acted under the name Richard Shannon and appeared in several Hollywood movies. "Jimmy was like the rainbow," he said. "You don't ever see one color; you see a maze of them. Nothing stands out in my memory of Jimmy but the bright light."

At the end of the year, hoping for bigger game, Dean decided to transfer to UCLA. To help pay his tuition Dean worked as an athletic instructor that summer at a boy's camp in Glendora, in the San Gabriel Valley, and in the fall of 1950 entered UCLA as a sophomore.

His major was now listed as theater arts, but again, perhaps as a compromise with his father, he took a cross section of academic courses: art history, geography, Latin American history, and general anthropology. He also took a course in basic air science as an Air Force ROTC cadet.

To help make friends on the large, sprawling campus, Dean went through rush week, and in September pledged a fraternity, Sigma Nu. He moved into the Sigma Nu house, a rambling Tudor-style dwelling on Gayley Avenue, and lived in a room with eight other pledges.

Jimmy wrote his aunt and uncle, telling them of his fraternity membership, and taking the opportunity to kid his uncle about UCLA's recent upset of Purdue. "You'll have to come West," he told him, "where they really play football."

At the fraternity house, Dean became friendly with Jim Bellah, son of novelist James Warner Bellah. Today a successful novelist himself, coauthor of the *Avenger Tapes*, Bellah was then a theater arts major who had transferred from Johns Hopkins. He was an ardent fencer and was trying to start a team at UCLA. Dean quickly took up the sport. "The first time he had a foil in his hand he damn near beat me," Bellah recalls. "He was the kind of guy who had to win. He had to be best at everything he did."

This spirit, however, did not endear him to some of the other brothers, and soon they and Dean were at odds. Dean was criticized for skipping pledge meetings and being chronically late for meals. Manuel Gonzales, the chapter president, who later became a corporate lawyer, remembered: "He spent a great deal of time in individual endeavors rather than taking part in any cohesive activities. Apparently, he was not comfortable in our group." A less articulate brother dismissed Jimmy simply as "a hick."

Matters came to a head one day when Dean got into a shoving match with another member. Dean later apologized and the incident was temporarily smoothed over, but it was obvious that the Indianan's days at the Sigma Nu house were numbered. Jim Bellah, who remained friends with Dean throughout his short life, later delivered this verdict: "He was a nice guy but fucked-up."

In early October, after a week of auditions, Dean was chosen to play Prince Malcolm in a campus production of *Macbeth*. He described this as "the biggest thrill of my life" in a letter to his aunt and uncle, proudly informing them the play would have almost a week-long run. "God! It's a dream," he wrote. "Don't anyone wake me up."

The part was not large, but it was important, and Dean threw himself into it with his customary enthusiasm—earning the customary response from his fellow actors. "He was ego-centric...," one complained. "He wouldn't act *with* the rest of us. He always pretended that he was alone on stage." Dr. Walden Boyle, the chairman of the theater arts department, who directed the production, was more understanding. In 1973, he reflected, "As I recall, Jim...had not had much acting training when he came to us. I suspect he found out that the university wasn't what he wanted. He wanted and needed a strong conservatory-type training and I believe he received that at the Actors Studio. When he was with us, he already had a fine presence on stage, but was disturbed, or perhaps bewildered, at not receiving more attention and direction than I could afford to give him in the part."

Rehearsals began on Thursday, October 12. The play opened at the Royce Hall Auditorium on November 29 and ran through December 2, 1950. Jimmy proudly noted that the hall sat sixteen hundred people. Tickets for evening performances cost $1.20, matinee seats were sixty cents.

Reviewing the production in the December issue of *Campus Theater Spotlight*, the organ of the theater arts department, critic Harve Bennett Fischman, a former radio Quiz Kid, expressed great disappointment. Fischman wrote: "Void of exciting movement, actor thought processes, and overall conception, the production neither snapped, crackled, nor popped. It just laid there."

Dean's own notice was buried toward the bottom of the page. It was brief and to the point: "Malcolm failed to show any growth and would have made a hollow king." Dean, however, saw things in a different light. Writing to his aunt and uncle in December, he informed them: "The play was very much of a success....I was very much rewarded and proved myself a capable actor in the eyes of several hundred culture-minded individuals. Man, if I can keep this up, and nothing interferes with my progress, one of these days I might be able to contribute something to the world (theatrically)."

One evening during rehearsals for *Macbeth* Dean had met William Bast, another student in the theater arts department, who had dropped by to pick up his girlfriend. At first, Bast later recalled, he barely took notice of his new friend; he had seen Dean on stage and had hardly been impressed by his slouching posture and Indiana drawl. James Dean: a name to forget, he decided.

Over coffee, however, the two got to know each other better and discovered their common background. Both were from the Midwest and transfer students. After two years at the University of Wisconsin, Bast had come to UCLA, hoping, like Dean, to become an actor.

By the time *Macbeth* completed its brief campus run, they were fast friends. It was a friendship that lasted until Dean's death and which Bast recounted in a long and engaging memoir (*James Dean*, Ballantine Books, 1956).

The two decided to share an apartment off campus, a small three-room flat that Bast had accidentally happened upon one afternoon. As soon as he showed it to Dean, they agreed to take it. To the relief of his fraternity brothers, James Dean moved his belongings out of the Sigma Nu house that same afternoon. It was later discovered he left an unpaid bill of forty-five dollars. One of Dean's fraternity brothers, Jim Bellah, also didn't care for Bast, whom he considered effeminate, and who "seemed to have his feet firmly planted in the air."

The apartment was conveniently close to campus. Located

on the top floor of an old Spanish-style house, it had a slanted, beamed ceiling that sloped from one end of the apartment to the other. There was a chest-high kitchen sink, designed in hand-laid Italian tile, and even a small redwood bar. The decor was all carefully chosen by the landlady, a middle-aged woman with a master's degree in art from the University of West Virginia.

Her new tenants quickly put these facilities to good use. Girls from the theater department were invited over to share home-cooked meals, sometimes dining to soft music and candlelight. Things were definitely on the upswing. Frequently, Bast recalled, these informal gatherings lasted well into the night, and one memorable get-together ended when the boys and their dates decided on a whim to drive ninety miles up the coast to have breakfast in Santa Barbara. On the way back the car broke down and they were stranded for several hours along the scenic highway overlooking the Pacific.

All this took its toll on their studies, and the boys' attendance records, which at best had been haphazard, grew worse. As the semester neared its end and exams approached, both Dean and Bast realized they were in serious academic trouble.

Bast was determined to buckle down and get through the welter of term papers and exams that suddenly faced him. Jimmy continued to let things slide. "I wanted to be a professional actor," he said later. "I couldn't take that tea-sipping...academic bull." He was undoubtedly telling the truth. The only professor listed on Dean's official transcript, Dr. Joseph B. Birdsell, his anthropology teacher, claims to have no recollection of "a James Dean" as ever having been among his students.

In January, Dean wisely decided to withdraw from college, a decision with which university officials concurred. Yet, once his decision to leave school had been made, Dean's spirits lifted. Now, at last, he could dedicate himself to becoming an actor.

"I don't want to be just a good actor," he told Bast

determinedly. "I don't even want to be the best. I want to grow, grow so tall nobody can reach me."

Through Jim Bellah, Dean met an independent theatrical agent, Isabelle Draesmer, who had a small office on Sunset Strip. She agreed to take Dean on as a client. She was not the biggest agent in Hollywood, but she was his. Furthermore, in the last few weeks of school Dean's father had gotten him a car: a slightly beat-up and dilapidated 1939 Chevrolet. It was not the sleekest of vehicles, but it ran. And now it would get him to auditions.

Dean's first professional job came deceptively easily. Bellah had heard of a television producer who needed some kids for a Pepsi commercial and invited his friend to come along. The commercial was shot in Griffith Park. Dean and the others rode around on a carousel, smiling contentedly. When the director said he also needed an actor to jitterbug in another sequence, Jimmy stepped forward and demonstrated his technique. He got the job and was paid twenty-five dollars to dance around a jukebox with a pretty girl and a guy named Nick Adams, who later appeared with him in *Rebel Without a Cause*.

In the evenings, Dean started to attend a drama workshop that had been organized by actor James Whitmore at Bill Bast's suggestion.

Whitmore had come to Hollywood after a successful career on Broadway, where he had appeared in the play *Command Decision*. Earlier he had studied at the Actors Studio and had developed a great admiration and respect for its cofounder, Elia Kazan. In Hollywood, Whitmore missed both the mental stimulation of New York and the opportunity to seriously study his own art. The idea of starting a class in which he could help young actors to grow, as well as sharpen his own skills, appealed to him at once.

Whitmore's class was informal. Students and teacher met two or three times a week, using an abandoned meeting room above the Brentwood Country Mart as a classroom.

"Acting is a craft, a serious profession," Whitmore told his young charges, "and to learn any craft you have to apply yourself. It takes time, study, practice....If it's glory you're after, you won't find it learning to act."

Much of the classwork was rudimentary: concentration techniques, improvisations, all the basic exercises. But for the first time Dean and the others became aware that acting was not merely a form of masquerading; it was a process that required them to think and feel deeply.

"You have to work at being an actor," Whitmore kept repeating. "Work until you're ready to drop, and then go on and work some more."

For one improvisation, Dean did a pine tree caught in a storm; he did another together with Bast, in which Dean played a thief who is trapped by a wary jeweler in his store. After an initial unsuccessful run-through, the two did the scene again, this time becoming so involved in their roles they almost came to blows and had to be restrained by other students.

Meanwhile, life back at the penthouse continued apace. Bast was in school again and also working part-time at CBS as an usher to help pay his tuition and support himself. For Dean, each day was an endless round of activity: sessions with a photographer to assemble an actor's portfolio, meeting with his agent, auditions.

Even when their second month's rent payment fell due, and the boys were sobered by the dent it made in their resources, they managed to squeeze by without too much sacrifice; meals were more meager, but girls from the theater department were still invited over to share them; dining by candlelight now had even an added charm: It cut down on the utilities bill.

Then, after several discouraging weeks in which nothing came Dean's way, Draesmer sent him and Bellah to audition for a television film being made by the Jerry Fairbanks studio. The film, *Hill Number One*, had a religious theme, and Dean read for the part of John the Apostle, the youngest of Christ's disciples. The casting director was impressed enough to choose Dean at once; Bellah was cast as a Roman soldier. Dean rushed back to the apartment and told Bast the good news, almost tipsy with joy.

An hour-long film, *Hill Number One* was to be taped for local showing during the Easter holidays. It was sponsored by Father Peyton's Family Theater, a well-known Catholic organization whose slogan "The Family That Prays Together Stays Together" had become almost a national byword.

The film's plot combined religion and patriotism. A group of weary GIs in Korea are bombarding a difficult objective—Hill Number 46. During a lull in the battle, a chaplain appears on Easter Sunday and comforts them by narrating the story of Christ's crucifixion on Calvary (Hill Number One). After the chaplain tells of the Resurrection, the soldiers learn that Hill Number 46 has fallen and the battle has been won.

The cast was surprisingly noteworthy. Raymond Burr played the Apostle Peter, and Leif Erickson Pontius Pilate. Roddy McDowall was one of the GIs; Ruth Hussey and Gene Lockhart also had roles.

The director, Arthur Pierson, had done a number of Hollywood films, including *Dangerous Years,* which had helped launch the career of Marilyn Monroe.

As the day of shooting approached, Bast remembered, his friend's nervousness increased until it became almost impossible for anyone to be around him. "I sometimes had the feeling," Bast wrote, "that he thought that by talking about the job, or admitting that it even existed, he would lose it. Once or twice it seemed...that he was hoarding his pleasure and excitement for fear that I, or someone else, might steal it from him, if he left it unguarded."

The shooting, however, came off well, and the film was completed within the week the studio had allotted for it. Dean appeared in a number of scenes and was confident he had done a good job. Dressed in a flowing robe and headdress, he spoke his lines crisply and in a deep, theater-trained voice. In one scene, he lectured his fellow Apostles, "Surely, we did not spend these years following the Master to return again to our nets." There was no trace of that twang which later marked his film performances. Toward the end of the film, Dean delivered a speech in front of Christ's tomb and Arthur Pierson even complimented him on his handling of it. The director proudly recalled: "He gave a fine, simple, straightforward performance," adding ruefully: "A year later he was in New York learning to be a mumbling rebel."

Both Dean and his agent hoped that the film would lead to bigger and better offers, and in the week before it was aired Draesmer was busy urging various producers to watch her client's performance. But after the film's release no other offers materialized. The production received several respectful reviews in local papers, and a notice even appeared in *Variety*. It did not mention Dean's name.

The only recognition Dean received was a letter from a group of girls at Immaculate Heart High School in Los Angeles whose teacher had required them to watch the show. They were starting a James Dean fan club, they informed him, and wanted him to be present at their first meeting. Dean went to this meeting and several others the girls held in their homes before the club quietly disbanded due to lack of funds.

When no new job offers appeared, Jimmy fell into a state of depression. His remarkable self-confidence seemed shaken. He would sit in his room for hours, silently staring into space or gazing out the window at the treetops beyond. At night he took long walks alone, strolling down to the Venice Amusement Pier to watch the people or walk along the beach, sometimes not returning till dawn.

"If I had thought it difficult to communicate with him at other times," Bast wrote, "I had never known such lack of communication as existed during his fits of depression. For my own peace of mind I found it wise to ignore him, or avoid him completely, going on about my business."

## 3

AS SUMMER NEARED, the enchantment of life in the penthouse grew considerably thinner. The weather turned hot and sticky. The $150 Dean had received for *Hill Number One* was long since used up, and money now became a serious problem.

Girls from the theater department were no longer invited over for dinner. Meals sometimes consisted of a bowl of dry oatmeal mixed with jam preserves; there were days when the larder was completely empty.

Dean managed to overcome his depression sufficiently to resume looking for work. Each morning he would climb into his old Chevy and head into Hollywood, only to return at the end of the day with the same discouraging news. Casting directors told him bluntly he wasn't good-looking enough to make it in the movies, or claimed he was too short to be an actor. "How can you measure acting in inches?" Dean said savagely. "They're crazy."

Luckily, at this time Bill Bast's mother decided to come west for a short visit, and the boys welcomed her presence with open relief. For a week their refrigerator was stocked solid with food and the cupboard shelves groaned under the weight of newly bought groceries.

For the first time the apartment even appeared orderly, and each night the boys were served a sumptuous meal on the small redwood bar.

After Mrs. Bast departed, Dean decided to find a part-time

job to help meet expenses until work as an actor came along. "Jimmy...had grown pleasantly accustomed to the little luxuries in life, like food," Bast explained, "and wanted to do something to perpetuate the habits we had formed, like eating."

Bast heartily endorsed his friend's plan and even arranged an appointment with the head usher at CBS to see about a job. Dean talked to the man and was hired.

From his first day at work, however, Jimmy found himself in hot water with his new employers. He was overheard complaining about the braided uniform he was given to wear, calling it a "monkey suit," and seemed unable to accord the head usher the proper respect demanded by his rank.

After a week Dean was fired.

"About your friend...," Bast was later chided at CBS, "let me tell you..."

As Dean slipped quickly and happily back into the ranks of the unemployed, the boys' financial situation looked bleaker than ever. "Times were still hard," Bast wrote, "and getting harder." Furthermore, Bast was tired of supporting them both, and his resentment grew daily.

To make matters worse, Dean began to spend much of his ample leisure time with a pretty girl, Beverly Wills, to whom Bast had introduced him and whom he occasionally dated himself. The daughter of the popular comedienne Joan Davis, Beverly was seventeen and the star of her own weekly CBS radio program *Junior Miss*. She lived with her mother in a mansion in fashionable Bel Air.

Unfortunately, Miss Davis did not share her daughter's enthusiasm for Dean. "He'd walk into our living room," Beverly recalled in a March 1957 issue of *Modern Screen*, "and promptly slump down in my mother's favorite armchair, his foot dangling over the side, and sit like that for hours without saying a word. The only action we'd see out of him was when he'd reach for the fruit bowl. He was always hungry."

When Beverly learned that pot roast was Dean's favorite

dish, she arranged to have it whenever he stayed for dinner. They also went on picnics together, or spent days at the beach, where Jimmy enjoyed racing her small motorboat.

By now, Bast's patience with his friend had all but run out. Bills continued to pour in with the speed of an avalanche, and in an effort to keep things going Bast had been borrowing money from whomever he could. "I was losing friends by the gross," he complained.

Perhaps hoping to placate his friend, Dean sometimes invited him along on the frequent outings he and Beverly enjoyed. When Beverly's mother gave her a large party to celebrate her eighteenth birthday, Bast was invited to attend.

The party turned out to be one of the social events of the summer for Hollywood's younger set. Debbie Reynolds, then a promising ingenue at MGM, was there, and so was Lugene Saunders, who was starring in a popular television series. Apparently young Jimmy didn't make much of an impression on Miss Reynolds. Although they were photographed together, Debbie later claimed she "never knew James Dean."

Bast arrived at the party late from work, feeling tired and out of place among the well-dressed guests. Dean appeared to be enjoying himself, mingling freely with the others.

A former national archery champion had been hired to entertain and was giving a daring exhibition of marksmanship.

Bast sat down alone by the pool, watching as the archer proceeded to break a balloon a volunteer held at arm's length.

The applause no sooner died down than Dean stepped forward, boldly challenging the man to shoot an apple off his head in the manner of William Tell. It was a stunt Miss Davis immediately prohibited as too dangerous.

Dean looked disappointed. Bast's heart sank; for one brief moment he had been hoping the archer might miss his target and nick his friend, nick him only slightly, but nick him just the same.

Several days later the inevitable finally occurred: After another argument over money erupted, Bast decided to move out. He found a room close to the CBS building and gave his new landlady a small deposit.

Jimmy was now on his own, left to enjoy alone the delights of penthouse living, complete with chest-high kitchen sink, Mexican oil portraits, and the rent that went with them.

To Bast's surprise, Dean managed rather well. He borrowed enough money from Beverly to pay some of his bills and began looking for a job, as simple as that.

Through Ted Avery, another disgruntled former usher at CBS, he found a job parking cars on a lot adjacent to the studio. The lot was a haven for out-of-work actors, run by a sympathetic man who allowed his young attendants to take off whenever they needed to go to auditions. The arrangement was ideal for Dean: The CBS executives who used the lot tipped well, bringing his salary almost to that of a full-time job. The hours were good, the work easy, and there was the ever-present chance that a producer or director might discover him.

By now, too, Dean's ability to live off newfound friends was almost a fine art, and before long he was sharing Avery's little Hollywood apartment rent free while the latter's wife was out of town.

An excellent horseman, Avery began teaching Dean how to ride and rope in the hope that Dean could obtain bit parts in cowboy movies as Avery sometimes did. The two of them were frequently seen in the staid corridors of CBS, twirling lariats and cutting up, dressed in full cowboy outfits.

Beverly Wills moved to Paradise Cove, by Malibu, for the rest of the summer, to be with her father, and she and Dean saw each other less often. The drive was too far for Dean to make regularly, and, moreover, he did not get along well with Beverly's new circle of friends, sensing they regarded him as an intruder in their exclusive suburban enclave.

Dean's unpredictability was also becoming upsetting to Beverly. "I learned," she later wrote, "that it was nothing for Jimmy to run through a whole alphabet of emotions in one evening, alternating sharply from low to high and back again, and no one could ever tell what mood would hit him."

At a dance one weekend Dean became jealous when another young man tried to dance with Beverly and almost started a fight. The incident embarrassed Beverly; she and Dean did not see each other for the rest of the summer. This pleased Joan Davis, Beverly's mother. "She couldn't think of any boy who had a less certain future than Jimmy," Beverly said. Years later, Beverly was killed in a fire, one of Dean's many friends—Nick Adams, Natalie Wood, Sal Mineo—who were to meet sad and tragic ends.

Freed from his ties to Beverly, Dean began to spend more time at the CBS studio, trying to cultivate whatever contacts he could. Although nothing came of Avery's plan to get them in westerns, through another friend Dean was introduced to Ralph Levy, an important TV director at CBS. The so-called King of Comedies, Levy was directing both the Allan Young and Ed Wynn shows for the network, and he used Dean as an extra whenever he could.

Levy claimed that even then Dean had a certain presence on stage, a magnetism that more than one person remarked upon. "People in the audience would tell me," the director said, "that when Dean was on stage they found their eyes going to him instead of the star of the show. There was no doubt of some electricity which transcended his innate talent."

Backstage, Levy gave the young actor encouragement and advice, and sometimes during a break in rehearsal the two adjourned to an alley behind the studio to toss around a baseball and talk.

At work on the lot Dean also met a number of other producers and directors, but it failed to lead to any acting jobs.

Then one Saturday morning he parked a car for a man named Rogers Brackett. When Dean learned that Brackett directed a weekly CBS radio program, *Alias Jane Doe*, starring Lurene Tuttle, he didn't waste any time confessing he was an actor. Over coffee, the two talked and Brackett casually promised to keep Dean in mind when casting future shows.

True to his word, he soon called Dean in to read for a small part. Dean's reading was melodramatic and his gestures overly theatrical for a radio studio, but Brackett awarded him the role. It was the first of six shows he did for Brackett. It was also the start of a long and invaluable friendship for Dean, but one that was not without its stormy moments. "I have often thought," Rogers later said, "I should have left 'Hamlet' in the parking lot."

A tall, curly-haired bachelor with good looks and an elegant manner, Brackett was some fifteen years Dean's senior. He was the son of Robert Brackett, an early Hollywood film producer who was once in partnership with Lewis J. Selznick. Born in Culver City, Brackett had literally been raised in Hollywood, and his connections in the film industry were numerous. He had served an apprenticeship with David O. Selznick, Lewis's son, and had worked at the Walt Disney Studio. He had left the film business to accept a high-paying position with the advertising firm of Foote, Cone, and Belding as account supervisor. One of his accounts sponsored *Alias Jane Doe,* and Brackett doubled as the show's director, an arrangement that was not uncommon.

At this time, Brackett was living at the Sunset Plaza, a fashionable apartment house above Sunset Strip.

When Ted Avery's wife returned to Hollywood, Dean was suddenly forced to find another place to live, and he accepted Brackett's invitation to stay with him.

For Dean, the Sunset Plaza proved a great improvement over Avery's modest quarters. Built on a hill, it afforded a majestic view of the city below. Brackett had a comfortable garden apartment that he was subletting from William Goetz, a Universal-International executive. The apartment was adjacent to the swimming pool.

Once again Jimmy had struck it rich—at a friend's expense. Through Brackett, too, Dean met a large number of people, and there was now glamour and excitement in his life. Rogers took him to private studio screenings, and they would dine at La Rue, a chic restaurant, where Dean liked the vichyssoise, always pronouncing it "swishy-swashy." During the day, Jimmy hung around the pool and took up photography. Often, he photographed himself in the mirror, a lifelong passion.

Rogers gave him books to read by writers like Saint-Exupéry and Camus, and introduced him to a movie house on Fairfax that showed silent films. Dean absorbed all this excitedly, asking for more. "He sapped the minds of his friends," Bast once noted, "like a bloodsucker saps the strength of an unsuspecting man."

But Dean's intelligence was largely intuitive, Brackett felt. He amazed Rogers with his ability to do mime, though he had never seen a performance. Once Dean surprised him by making a mobile, using wire and some chicken bones that had been left over from dinner the night before. When Rogers told him how much he liked the mobile, Jimmy answered, "What's a mobile?"

Soon Rogers was pretty hung up on his young friend, and they drifted into an affair. "My primary interest in Jimmy was as an actor—his talent was so obvious," Brackett said. "Secondarily, I loved him, and Jimmy loved me. If it was a father-son relationship, it was also somewhat incestuous."

One afternoon Jim Bellah dropped by to see Dean. He was taken aback by his fraternity brother's new living arrangements. Brackett was polished, droll, clever. Bellah found him "terribly precious." It was definitely not his scene. When Rogers left the room, Bellah turned to Jimmy and said, "This guy's a fairy." Dean replied: "Yeah, I know."

Was this merely a convenient relationship for Dean? After all, the casting couch was as much a part of Hollywood as the tall palms and wide boulevards. Jimmy would not be the first to use or to be used. Other legends have their little secrets.

Rogers himself sometimes wondered about the depth of

Dean's emotion. Long after their friendship ended, he vividly recalled coming home one evening and finding Jimmy sitting in their bedroom crying. When he asked what was the matter, Dean said cryptically, "I can't love and I can't be loved." But Rogers maintained their sex life was not one-sided. In an interview in the 1970s, he said he believed their physical relationship had been mutually satisfying.

A brilliant stage director, Brackett had had the first Equity company in California, and he began to coach Dean in plays and readings. They rehearsed *Hamlet* on the grand staircase of the Sunset Plaza, overlooking the pool. "Elsinor with room service," Rogers quipped. Then, for contrast, Dean would recite some poems by James Whitcomb Riley he had learned as a boy. " 'Little Orphant Annie' was quite one of his favorites," Brackett remembered. "It was very funny and very touching...."

As the war in Korea heated up and Uncle Sam needed soldiers, Dean was called for induction. "Deploring that and any other war," Brackett advised Dean to get out of the draft. "Better the funeral pyre in his Porsche than Korea," Brackett later said. "With his quasi-jock predilections he'd never have made it back...I feel."

Through a doctor friend, Brackett set up an appointment with a psychiatrist for Dean. After a viable number of sessions, the shrink came up with a document "that cooled the draft board." Years later, in 1974, Rogers wrote frankly in a letter: "As Jimmy was 'living' with me, there was no question that his unsuitability for military service was valid, or so they were led to believe. It's one thing in the relationship he never regretted." According to his Selective Service System Record, Dean was classified "IV-F." When the actor saw Bellah and broke the news of his deferment, he told him, "I kissed the doctor."

Dean's contact with his family had been minimal since leaving UCLA. When he and Rogers visited them in their home in the Valley to pick up some clothes, Dean discovered that to earn extra cash his father was raising chinchillas in a spare bedroom. Rogers thought the scene was something out of *The Day of the Locust,* Nathanael West's novel about people down on their luck in dreamland California. Conversation was strained all the way around.

Along with David Wayne, the actor, and his wife, Dean and Rogers went to Tijuana for a weekend to see a bullfight, first staying overnight in Laguna. Another time, Dean traveled with Brackett to Mexicali where they saw the matador Arruza in the ring. In Mexicali Jimmy met Budd Boetticher, a movie director and bullfight aficionado who had served as technical adviser for the film *Blood and Sand.* Boetticher gave Dean a blood-stained cape that had once belonged to Sidney Franklin, the Brooklyn-bred matador who had achieved fame in the rings of Spain and about whom Hemingway had written.

The cape became Dean's prize possession and, thereafter, wherever he traveled, the cape traveled with him.

Because of Brackett's many friends in the movie business, Jimmy easily found work as an extra. He made his film debut in Paramount's *Sailor Beware,* a Dean Martin–Jerry Lewis comedy. In a boxing sequence, Dean acted as a second for Jerry Lewis's opponent. A white towel draped around his neck, Dean spoke his first words on the Silver Screen: "That guy's a professional."

He next appeared in a Korean War movie, *Fixed Bayonets,* starring Richard Basehart, and directed by Samuel Fuller, a friend of Brackett's. Again, Dean had one line of dialogue: "It could be the rear guard coming back." "What a part," he later said.

At Universal-International he had two days' work playing a teenager in another comedy, *Has Anybody Seen My Gal?,* starring Rock Hudson and Piper Laurie. In the film, Dean comes into an ice cream parlor and orders an elaborate ice cream sundae. The counterman, played by Charles Coburn, asks him to come back the next day for a fitting. Dean described the film as "family-type" entertainment.

It was not until years later, when the film was shown on television, that Piper Laurie learned she had once made a movie with James Dean.

Not all of Brackett's friends liked Dean, however, or were anxious to advance his career. A meeting Rogers arranged with Leonard Spiegelgass, a story editor at MGM and an important man in the studio hierarchy, ended in disaster when Spiegelgass ordered Dean from his house. "His manners were terrible," Spiegelgass said. "He flicked ashes on the rug and behaved like an animal. The boy was absolute poison." Spiegelgass warned Brackett that he was "ruining his reputation" by pushing Dean so hard, but Brackett paid no attention.

At the Zuma Beach home of George Bradshaw, the short story writer, Dean accidentally set fire to one of Bradshaw's favorite armchairs and Brackett had to pay for its repair.

"Jimmy was like a child," Brackett said. "He behaved badly just to get attention." But he added, "He was a kid I loved— sometimes parentally, sometimes not parentally."

Like a child, too, Dean seemed to be forever testing the affection of those closest to him. "The only way he could be sure you really loved him," another friend, Stewart Stern, later said, "was if you loved him when he was truly at his worst."

By the fall Dean was becoming slightly bored with the life he was leading. He sought out his old friend Bill Bast, whom he had hardly seen since the penthouse fiasco in midsummer. Bast was now working as a pageboy on several shows at CBS and preparing to start his senior year at UCLA.

"You know," Dean confided to him, "it gets sickening. The other day we were sitting at the pool and I made a bet with Rogers that the names of La Rue or the Mocambo would be dropped at least fifteen times within the next hour. We kept count and I won. What a pile of..."

As always, whatever the state of his personal life, Dean's career was foremost in his mind, and he again was worried about his future as an actor. "A guy could go on knocking his brains out, getting nothing but bit parts for years," he told Bast over a bowl of chili at Barney's Beanery. "There's got to be more."

To another struggling actor, Dean confessed the same fear. "They'll never give me a real chance out here," he said. "I'm not the bobby-sox type, and I'm not the romantic leading-man type either. Can you imagine me making love to Lana Turner?"

Although he was attending James Whitmore's class less regularly, his respect for the actor remained as great as ever. When Whitmore took him aside after class one evening and spoke to him sharply, Dean listened. "Stop dissipating your energy and talent," Whitmore urged. He told him to "quit just hanging around Hollywood" and go to New York where he would be able to study and master his craft. "Learn to be an actor. It doesn't take anything if all you want to be is just another ham."

Later, in press interviews with Hedda Hopper and others, Dean would credit Whitmore with stimulating his interest in serious acting and encouraging him to go to New York. Although Whitmore no doubt did influence him, Dean never publicly mentioned his real mentor, Rogers Brackett, or acknowledged the help he had generously given. But if Dean had any lingering doubts about leaving, they were dispelled when Rogers was called to Chicago, the home office of Foote, Cone, & Belding, on an important assignment. Eventually, Brackett hoped to be transferred to New York, but he had no idea how many months he might have to remain in Chicago. For the third time in three short months Dean was about to literally lose the roof over his head. It proved to be too much.

"I can't stomach this dung hole anymore," he told Bast with finality after a late-night talk session.

Several days later, when Bast returned to his apartment after work, he found a message the landlady had left: "Mr. Dean called. Gone to New York."

**4**

BEFORE ARRIVING IN NEW YORK, Jimmy stopped off in Chicago to see Rogers Brackett, who was staying at the Ambassador East. Brackett remembers Dean made quite a stir striding through the lobby of the expensive hotel dressed in blue jeans, and carrying his bullfighter's cape slung over his shoulder. After about a week in the Windy City, Dean visited the Reverend DeWeerd for a few days at his new home in Indianapolis and paid a visit to the farm to see his aunt and uncle. Then he proceeded on his journey.

In New York, Dean took a room at the Iroquois Hotel on West 44th Street, several blocks from Times Square. It was October 1951.

"New York frightened and overwhelmed me," Dean said afterward. "For the first few weeks I barely strayed from my hotel. I would see three movies a day to ease the loneliness I felt."

Gradually, as his fears subsided, he began to explore the city around him. He took his first subway ride and went on long walks, once wandering as far as South Ferry, near the Battery. There were nights, he later said, when he walked up and down Broadway alone, wondering if he would ever make it.

He made a friend, Harry Drake, a young would-be artist who had grown up on a wheat farm in Kansas. The two delved into the big city together, visiting libraries and museums. They

searched secondhand bookstores along Eighth Avenue, looking for old bullfight posters, and discovered Hector's, an
inexpensive Times Square cafeteria, known for its glazed
cakes. Drake was an amateur photographer and Dean sometimes borrowed his equipment and spent the day photographing sights around the city.

In a very real way, Dean was completing his education,
learning from all that lay around him. "New York is generous,"
he once said, "and above all fertile...."

Jimmy had been given money by the Reverend DeWeerd,
Brackett, and the Winslows for his trip. He had also saved up a
few dollars from his movie work and had sold his car; but even
so, his resources probably amounted to no more than five
hundred dollars. When this was nearly gone, Dean got a job
washing dishes in a tavern on West 45th Street. To economize
he took a small room at the YMCA on West 63rd Street, just a
short block from Central Park.

Before leaving Los Angeles, Dean had been given the
names of several people to look up, and he now decided to get
in touch with them. He called James Sheldon, an advertising
executive who was a friend of Ralph Levy's, and made an
appointment to see him. He also phoned one of Brackett's
friends, Alec Wilder, the composer who had written such
popular tunes as "I'll Be Around" and "Who Can I Turn To?"
and Wilder invited him over to the Algonquin Hotel, where he
then lived. "Rogers had already warned me," Wilder recounted, "to be on the lookout for 'this real wild kid,' but Dean
was polite at our initial meeting. I suppose he was so new in
town he had to be well behaved."

Dean's first meeting with Sheldon turned out well, too. A
big, friendly man, then in his late twenties, Sheldon was
working as account supervisor at Young & Rubicam, hoping to
eventually break into television as a director.

Through his contacts at the agency, Sheldon had heard that
the young actor (Dick Van Patten) who played Nels on the
popular TV series *Mama* was about to be drafted into the army,

and the network was worried about a replacement. Sheldon thought Dean would be perfect; he had seen the Broadway play *I Remember Mama*, on which the series was based, and Dean reminded him very much of the actor who had played Nels on the stage, a young midwesterner named Marlon Brando.

Sheldon contacted Doris Quinlain, the show's coproducer, and sent Dean over to read. Years later, the director, Ralph Nelson, recalled: "Since the series was a very successful one, we naturally wanted to replace [Van Patten] with the best possible young actor we could find. It proved more difficult than expected. Those actors with talent were homosexuals of such a degree that we did not dare use them on the air, or they were young and manly, [but] lacked the talent that was required. Finally, Miss Quinlain came up with a young man who was not only handsome and talented, but seemed very sincere about his work—although a little bit strange in his approach to it. His name was James Dean."

Nelson decided to ease Dean into the role. He was first used in a number of bit parts—walk-on roles. At first it appeared Dean would be an excellent choice to play the teenage son in the saga about an immigrant family in early twentieth-century San Francisco. But during the brief trial period, Dean became increasingly uncooperative. "His surliness mounted," the director explained, and "the roles seemed beneath him." The director was also surprised that "the money was not important" to the young actor. As Nelson recalled, Dean actually played the part of Nels for a couple of weeks. Perhaps the role of the dutiful young son just did not appeal to him. But the director's dilemma was suddenly swept away when Van Patten failed his army physical and returned to the show. "I welcomed him with open arms," Nelson remembered, "and released Dean from any more involvement with the program."

Still anxious to help, Sheldon then introduced Dean to Jane Deacy, a theatrical agent at the Louis Shurr office. An able and intelligent woman, Miss Deacy had started as a switchboard operator at Shurr and worked her way up, becoming one of the office's top agents. Her clients included Gower Champion, the dancer, and Priscilla Gillette, who had played the lead in *Brigadoon* on Broadway. Later, she would guide the career of George C. Scott.

To this day, Miss Deacy steadfastly refuses to publicly discuss either her first meeting with Dean or their subsequent relationship. But another employee of the Shurr office recalled: "Jimmy appealed enormously to Jane's maternal instinct. He had that lonely-boy quality which women find irresistible. And, of course, she believed he had talent. Like all good agents, she almost has a sixth sense when it comes to finding actors.... From the very beginning her faith in Jimmy was utter and complete."

While Miss Deacy set about the task of finding him work, Dean did his best to keep body and soul together on his own.

Through another young actor he found part-time employment on the television game show *Beat the Clock*. Dean was paid five dollars an hour as a stand-in to test lighting and camera angles. He also tried out the show's stunts during rehearsals, in front of a live audience. Dean liked the work and always showed up for rehearsals on time. Unfortunately, his agility was such that he was able to do stunts that contestants later found impossible, and, after a while, producer Jean Hollander was forced to find another actor with less coordination.

When winter came, Dean still had not found any steady work as an actor, but his days were far from empty. He avidly followed the trade papers, hoping to come across parts he might audition for. Along with a young actress named Jeanne, whom he had met in the Astor drugstore, a favorite haunt of aspiring actors, Dean informally rehearsed scenes from a wide variety of plays. "He'd phone my apartment at the strangest times," Jeanne remembered, "and ask if it was okay to come by. It might be midnight or four in the afternoon, but when I said yes, he'd come right over, and we'd work together on a scene he had brought."

"Work, study," James Whitmore had told him. "Learn to be an actor." In his own way Dean was doing just that.

In January, Dean learned that Joan Davis and her daughter Beverly were in town. Miss Davis had come east to do a radio show with Tallulah Bankhead, and she and her daughter were staying at the Plaza. Forgetting the bad feeling of the summer before, Dean phoned Beverly and made a date for dinner.

Beverly was alarmed when she saw Dean: Despite the cold he was wearing the same thin blue jacket she remembered from the summer and a pair of dirty gray slacks. In his lapel he had a small matador's sword that he was especially proud of.

They ate in an Italian restaurant, and over dinner Dean sheepishly admitted he had been living largely on milkshakes since leaving Hollywood. Yet, throughout the evening he did his best to maintain an aura of bravado. When he took Beverly back to her hotel and they said good night, Dean promised her, "I'll show them."

Then he left, walking across the park to the little room he had at the Y.

On evenings when he was alone, Dean often dropped by the Rehearsal Club, looking for companionship. The club had been built in 1913 to serve as a residence for girls who came to New York seeking careers in show business. Residents were well chaperoned, and male visitors were only permitted in the lounge until the midnight curfew.

"Jimmy was always hanging around," a former resident said, "whether he had a date or not. The girls at the club all kind of adopted him. One girl I knew even gave him an old camel-hair coat she had worn in college. It was too small on him but he wore it anyway."

One rainy day Dean borrowed an umbrella from a girl sitting across from him in the lounge. It turned out she was a dancer named Elizabeth Sheridan, who had been living at the club for several months.

A couple of days later, Dean returned her umbrella. She was on her way to a dance rehearsal nearby and Dean went along to watch. "When I first met Jimmy," she later said, "he looked like a straggly, hungry kid who needed a friend. After, I found he always looked that way."

Of mixed Irish-Jewish ancestry, Dizzy, as everyone called her, was the daughter of Frank Sheridan, the classical pianist, and had grown up in Westchester. Another friend at the time described her as "a long, lithe, supple beauty with a pixie humor that came across in everything she said and did."

In her, Jimmy found a kindred spirit—almost a mirror image of himself. Lively and inquisitive, she wanted to be a dancer, a cowboy, a matador. Like Dean, she had left school against her family's wishes to pursue her career. Also like her newfound friend, she was very broke.

"We would sit and talk for hours and hours," Dizzy remembers, "getting to know each other better all the time." Sometimes Dean would call and play records for her over the phone. "It was a desperate feeling we had toward needing each other," Dizzy said, "and pretty soon we got to be inseparable."

They spent much of their time at Jerry's, a small Italian place on 54th Street, not far from the Rehearsal Club. There was a new drink called Champale they both liked, and the restaurant's proprietor, Jerry Lucce, allowed them to stay as long as they wanted over a single bottle. Sometimes, when Dean was broke, an easygoing waiter named Louie loaned him a few dollars or sneaked him a plate of spaghetti.

After Jerry's closed, Dean would take Dizzy to an Automat on Broadway that was open all night. "We'd sit there till the wee hours," Dizzy recalled, "talking about scripts or trees or bugs or anything and everything."

Dean told her his philosophy as an actor. "I don't care what sort of part they give me. If I get a part, even if it's washing dishes, I'll get a dishpan and wash and wash until my hands peel and I know exactly how it feels to wash dishes. That's the only way I can act."

"Lots of times," Dizzy remembers, "we used to walk along Fifth Avenue and look in store windows. Mostly it was cars. He was fascinated by cars. He always wanted a Jaguar and I always wanted a Jaguar and there was a place on Broadway up around the sixties, a great big store window that had all sorts of cars in it. We used to hang around and look in the window and dream about the Jaguar we were someday going to get. It turned out he got a Porsche, or it got him."

Dean copied a passage from his favorite book, *The Little Prince*, and pasted it in his actor's portfolio to comfort him as he made his rounds. His faith in himself remained as firm as ever. "He never for one instant doubted he would make it," Dizzy claimed. "I mean, he always knew that he would one day be a star, and there was no question in his mind about it at all."

Even with Dizzy, Jimmy indulged in his penchant for stories. All his life he flirted with fantasy, later telling a producer he had run with the bulls at Pamplona, bragging to a fellow actor he had been in jail. Once, he confided to Dizzy that he had met his hero, Saint-Exupéry, and that he was an "ugly old man who loved flying." It didn't matter that the dashing author was killed in 1944, missing on a wartime flight over the African desert while Dean was still a boy in Indiana.

When Dizzy and her new friend realized how much time they were spending in each other's company, they decided it would probably be just as easy to move in together. They found a room at the Hargrave Hotel on West 72nd Street, off Columbus Avenue. Their room was the size of a broom closet, Dizzy recalled, and the wallpaper was peeling off in layers. But they hung up a few drawings Dean had done in his sketchbook and called the place home.

Dean brought along a hotplate he had used to cook on at the Y, and he and Dizzy prepared simple meals on it. "He was always talking about steaks," Dizzy said, "how he loved good steaks…but in the early part of our relationship we didn't do much eating." Shredded wheat and milk dinners were a big part of their diet.

To avoid buying any new clothes they wore each other's spare blue jeans. On cold nights when the old radiator broke down, Dean's bullfighter's cape served as an extra blanket to keep them warm.

Jimmy taught Dizzy to sketch, telling her to look out the window and draw what she saw. One morning Dean had an early appointment with a casting agent, but before he left he made a hardboiled egg and left it on a table for Dizzy when she awakened. He drew a face on the egg and wrote a cheerful note.

"What I remember most about Jimmy was his gentleness," recalls Dizzy, a television and stage actress today, who is married to a composer. "Ours was a very private relationship. During the time we were together we saw as few other people as possible. It was the way both of us wanted it."

Early in February, Dean turned twenty-one. He and Dizzy celebrated at Jerry's, along with a few friends of hers from the Rehearsal Club. Dean told her it was the "best birthday he had in years."

A week later, Dean received a fitting, if belated, birthday present. Archer King, a young agent at the Shurr Office who worked closely with Jane Deacy, sent him to read for a part on *The Web*, a half-hour television mystery program. The role was that of a bellhop who helps solve his brother's murder at a plush mountain resort. "The minute he started reading," said Lela Swift, the director, "I knew that boy had something special."

Along with Anne Jackson, E. G. Marshall, and Robert Simon, Dean was cast in the show.

As soon as rehearsals began, however, Dean's temperament got him in trouble. Producer Franklin Heller found him "moody," "unresponsive to suggestions," "very difficult," "not on time," and "generally a pain in the ass." Had it not been for Miss Swift, who insisted on having him in the part, Dean probably would have been fired.

After a four-day rehearsal, the show ("Sleeping Dogs") was done live on February 20, 1952, a Wednesday. Even those who had been most skeptical were impressed by Dean's perfor-

A shot from the family
album: Jimmy at two

A smiling child

Infielder at Fairmount High School

On the basketball team at Santa Monica City College

As Prince Malcolm
in a 1950 UCLA
production of
*Macbeth*

Jimmy in New York

Prior to his
*East of Eden*
role

On a TV Easter program in Los Angeles

Playing with toy autos with his cousin

Getting attention at the Warner commissary

With Julie Harris on the *East of Eden* set
(PHOTOPLAY LETTERPRESS)

With Dick
Davalos in
*East of Eden*

With Bill
Bast's mother

Relaxing on the
*East of Eden* set

Jimmy and Debbie
Reynolds at the
Davis home
(PHOTOPLAY)

The aspiring actor

With Mildred
Dunnock in a
TV drama

Playing an Arab
blackmailer in
*The Immoralist*
on Broadway
(TIME INC.)

With director
Nicholas Ray
and Natalie Wood
on the set of *Rebel
Without a Cause*

A rebel
against society

The fight scene in *Rebel*

mance. "He gave us all a terrible time in rehearsal," Anne Jackson commented, "but on the air he was just marvelous." Franklin Heller went out of his way to tell Dean how good he had been. Dean murmured his thanks. "He was as gracious," Heller said later, "as Jimmy Dean could be."

Following his success, Dean was quickly signed to appear on another television show, *Martin Kane*, a private-eye series. In the show, Dean was to play a student who becomes mixed up in a homicide; the director selected him because he "seemed like a typical college kid." Once again, rehearsals had no sooner started than Dean was at odds with the rest of the cast, and this time with the show's director, Frank Burns, as well. "No one knew what was coming up next," Burns complained. To steady Dean in rehearsal, Burns told him, "Be yourself," but in retrospect, the director recalled this was probably unsound advice, since he "didn't know what 'yourself' meant to Dean at that time."

"Dean was a very inventive actor," explained Edgar Kahn, another director at the studio. "But in those days television shows were 'shot tight.' The emphasis was on getting the job done as quickly and cheaply as possible. There wasn't enough time for the constant probing of a part Dean liked."

After several warnings, Dean was fired by director Burns; the show had been in rehearsal only two days.

When Dean returned to the Shurr office and Archer King asked for an explanation, Dean told him curtly: "I was trying to get a characterization. I couldn't worry about going to some damn chalk mark." The novice was proud of his independence. Later, in Hollywood, Dean told another actor how he had stood up to the director. "Don't be afraid to keep them waiting," he said.

His television career temporarily sidetracked, Dean turned to Dizzy, relying on her to get him through the blue periods he fell prey to.

Since their hotel was close to Central Park, they would go there in the afternoons when the weather was mild. Dean liked to take along his sketchbook and bullfighter's cape. To take his mind off everything, he practiced his capework by the hour while Dizzy watched, or sketched, or read; his audience of one. Sometimes they rode on the park's carousel, like any kid and his special girl.

When their money finally ran out, Dizzy went to work as a retoucher for the American Photograph Corporation, and Dean took whatever jobs he could. He worked as an extra on *Tales of Tomorrow,* a science fiction show, and landed a bit part on *Studio One.* Once again, Dean played a bellhop. The show, "Ten Thousand Horses Singing," starred John Forsythe and a lovely actress named Catherine McLeod. The future screen legend had one line of dialogue: "Yes, sir," crisply spoken in the hotel lobby.

During this time, Dean grew closer to Jane Deacy, his agent, frequently visiting the Yorkville apartment where she lived with her husband, a radio engineer, and their young son. To help Jimmy out, Miss Deacy would slip him five dollars or so, telling him when he became a star he could pay her back. Dean now called her Mom.

Dean introduced Dizzy to Alec Wilder, and the composer of "While We're Young" entertained them at the Algonquin over tea. Wilder liked Dizzy at once. "She was a wonderful girl," Wilder said, "and an extremely good influence for Dean. He needed her. Whenever she was with him, he was calmer and more stable than usual."

Toward the end of the winter Dizzy took Jimmy to Larchmont to meet her family, and then the two of them drove to Connecticut for a day, visiting Daycroft, Dizzy's old school.

In late March their funds ran out again, and they were forced to move out of their hotel. Dizzy found a tiny room on Eighth Avenue, and Dean went to live with Rogers Brackett, who had come to New York several months earlier. In fact, he and Jimmy had spent Christmas together at an inn in Garrison, New York. Rogers later remembered it as an "old fashioned country Christmas." Still working for Foote, Cone, & Belding, he was now with their Madison Avenue office and had a loft apartment on West 38th Street, just off Fifth Avenue near Lord & Taylor, the fashionable department store.

As in the past, Brackett was only too glad to help his young protégé. One of the accounts he handled was the Hallmark Company, which sponsored the *Hallmark Hall of Fame,* and by pulling a few strings he got them to hire Dean.

For his paycheck each week, Dean was required to do little more than show up at the studio; the only actual duty he had was to stand at a blackboard and list the show's credits as the program went off the air. This was done live and in close-up, showing only Dean's hand on camera. But even to this Jimmy was able to bring a flair that was all his own: invariably as he got to the final words "devised and directed by Albert McCleery," he would either break the chalk or scrape it in such a way as to make an unpleasant noise.

Albert McCleery was never sure whether this was accidental or not, but because of Brackett he was forced to put up with Dean anyway.

For Dean, life now seemed curiously happy. He and Dizzy were still together much of the time, but there were again gay times with Rogers too: evenings spent at the ballet or dining in expensive restaurants. One night, Rogers remembered, he and Jimmy saw William Faulkner hanging around the Algonquin lobby. But, for a change, Jimmy was too tongue-tied to introduce himself to the great author.

Dizzy knew of Dean's relationship with Brackett and it caused her great pain. She claimed that her "woman's intuition" had sensed it. Over twenty years later, she was reluctant to talk about the director out of loyalty to her dead friend. In a way, Dizzy rationalized Brackett's presence by believing Jimmy's claim that he had originally come to New York "to get away from Brackett," but that the director had "pursued" him.

On one occasion she met Brackett and was noticeably cold, if not outright rude, to him. Later, Jimmy gave her a hug and thanked her for "standing up to Rogers."

On Sunday nights, after the Hallmark telecast, Sarah Churchill, the show's hostess, held open house for the cast at her penthouse on Central Park South, and Dean and Brackett always went. To entertain her guests Miss Churchill did imitations of her father, Sir Winston, and told amusing stories of what it had been like being the prime minister's daughter.

Dean seemed almost star struck by these gatherings and was fond of Miss Churchill, who would take him aside and lecture him good-naturedly about his behavior, especially the tricks he played on Albert McCleery.

As if to underscore his present good fortune, Dean got a lead on the *U.S. Steel Radio Hour,* playing a friend of Abe Lincoln—one of Jimmy's own heroes—in "Prologue to Glory." He worked with John Lund and Wanda Hendrix, both already well-established actors.

Lund was taken both by Dean's "exceptional talent" and his casual manner. Decades later, he remembered how Jimmy "always addressed me as 'Abe'—on or away from the microphone." He also recalled that the young thespian "had a way of sitting apart and smiling a secret smile as though in response to some droll story that only he could hear."

If Dean was pleased with himself, no one could blame him: After all, appearing on national radio was not a bad way for an Indiana farmboy to mark his first six months in New York City.

Then, as winter finally ended and spring filled the air, Dean heard some more good news: Another old friend was coming to New York.

William Bast had written, saying that as soon as he graduated, he planned to come east to live, and he promised to look Dean up the very moment he got to town.

# 5

DURING BILL BAST'S first week in New York, Dean gave him what amounted to an orientation program. He took him on his acting rounds, showed him the sights of the city, and introduced him to people.

Bast was struck by the poise and self-assurance Dean had acquired; no longer was he the frightened young man, unsure of his future, that Bast remembered. He now seemed confident and more determined, and Bast could feel it.

"I've discovered a whole new world here," Dean told him, "A whole new way of thinking.... This town's the end. It's talent that counts here. You've got to stay with it or get lost. I like it."

Because of his past experiences, Bast easily found a job with CBS, working in the communications department. He had already given up the idea of becoming an actor and, instead, hoped to write, either novels or short stories. Until he became more firmly settled, he took a room at the Iroquois.

Dizzy was offered a job in stock in Ocean City, New Jersey, as an assistant choreographer, and decided to take it. Dean left Brackett's apartment and moved in with Bast.

Jimmy now decided to do something he had long planned on: audition for the Actors Studio, the famed workshop conducted by Lee Strasberg and Elia Kazan. Dean had first heard of the school through James Whitmore, who encouraged him to seek admittance, but until now, he had not felt he was ready.

Then at the height of its prestige, the Studio had helped train such actors as Marlon Brando, Montgomery Clift, Geraldine Page, and Ben Gazzara. It had a mystique that no other acting school would ever equal. As one observer put it, the Studio served as "a home, a school," and a "psychoanalytic couch" all rolled into one.

For his audition Dean decided to team up with Christine White, a young actress who was also a client of Jane Deacy's. Jimmy met her one afternoon when he stoped by the office. In fact, Archer King had encouraged him to hang out at the place as much as he liked—"since he was less apt to get in trouble."

Blonde and petite, Chris was from Washington, D.C., and had studied English literature at the University of North Carolina. She was then sharing a cramped apartment on 92nd Street and Madison Avenue with several college friends.

Before coming to New York, Chris had acted in summer stock on Cape Cod, and she had arrived in the city only a few weeks earlier. She had come by seaplane, a fact that intrigued Dean immediately.

"Jimmy was an impulsive, immediate creature," remembers Chris, who later won acclaim in *A Hat Full of Rain* on Broadway. "He could look at a delicatessen window and suddenly start waving at a bowl of prunes like they were alive. He was childish in a charming way."

The scene they chose was one that Chris had written. It ran for seven pages and involved an encounter on a beach between an intellectual drifter and an aristocratic Southern girl.

In order to get the proper outdoors feeling, Dean insisted they rehearse in the open, either in Central Park or on the sunroof of Chris's apartment building.

Over a period of several months they shaped and molded the scene. Whenever inspiration struck, Jimmy jotted down notes or comments on the original typescript until, according to Chris, it "resembled an instruction sheet on how to make a sofa."

They tried out the scene in front of Bast and Chris's roommates, and to get the reactions of others Jimmy would stop strangers in the park and ask them to watch.

Despite their preparation, on audition day Dean was understandably nervous. They had brought along a bottle of beer as a prop, but in his excitement Dean drank the bottle and had to run out for another.

Finally their turn came. As the scene opened, Dean was supposed to be gazing at the stars, speculating about a coming hurricane. "Well," Chris remembers, "Jimmy couldn't see a thing without his glasses. He couldn't even find center stage. And he couldn't even find me when I made my entrance. But every line came out clear."

Usually Studio auditions are limited to five minutes, at the end of which time the judges ring a bell. But when Chris and Dean ran several minutes over the allotted time, they were not interrupted. Strasberg found the simple scene "natural and very believable." Dean made "a wonderful impression" on him.

Out of the 150 who auditioned only fifteen were accepted; both Dean and Christine White were among them. At twenty-one, Jimmy was one of the youngest members ever to be admitted.

That night he elatedly took Chris to Jerry's for dinner, and, as an encore, they did their scene for Jerry Lucce.

Encouraged by his achievement, Dean got to work at once on Studio projects. He and Chris improvised a scene about a young married couple planning a trip; as they looked over a map, their chatter revealed their relationship.

Jimmy had recently read and liked a novel by Barnaby Conrad, *Matador*, and decided to dramatize a chapter from it. The book is about an aging matador whose pride forces him to accept a challenge from a young rival even though it means almost certain death.

Dean wanted to convey the man's emotions as he prepares for the final fight. The acting was to be an internal monologue, done without words, and using only a few props: a statue of the Virgin, a candle, and the matador cape.

Once again, Dean worked hard to get his work ready. "When he prepared an acting job," Bast said, "he put his heart and soul into it."

The performance was done in front of a full session of the Studio, presided over by Lee Strasberg.

A small, catlike man, Strasberg was then already a living legend, known as the founder of the so-called Method school of acting, based on the theories of the Russian director Konstantin Stanislavski. According to the Method, actors were encouraged to draw on their own past experiences to project themselves emotionally in a role.

As a teacher, Strasberg's criticisms were often sharp and abrasive, his manner rather formal. Students called him "the Archbishop." Some at the Studio compared his technique of taking apart an actor's performance to that of a surgeon cutting away bad tissue; others said the whole process was more like being raked over hot coals.

Always sensitive to criticism, Dean was not ready for the sharp critique Strasberg launched into. "What are you trying to show us?" the director asked, telling Dean that he had performed "an exercise—not a scene." Supposedly Eli Wallach and Marilyn Monroe were in the audience. Dean was very embarrassed. As Chris White recalled, "Jimmy's face turned ashen," and when Strasberg finished speaking, Dean threw his bullfight cape over his shoulder and walked out without saying a word.

"I don't know what's inside of me," he told Bill Bast. "I don't know what happens when I act....But if I let them dissect me like a rabbit in a laboratory I might not be able to produce again.

"That man had no right to tear me down like that. You keep knocking a guy down like that and you take the guts away from him. And what's an actor without guts?"

Angered and hurt, for a long time Dean swore he would never return to the Studio.

As summer crept upon the city, so did the annual show-business hiatus, the time when television programs went off the air and theaters closed their doors, leaving actors to sweat out the muggy New York summer.

In July the Hallmark show suspended its programming until the fall, and Dean's sinecure came to an abrupt end. "Like a variation on an old theme," Bast wrote, "money soon became a major problem again. It was a common occurrence for us to divide the sixty or seventy cents we might have between us to buy a slim dinner at the Automat." Lunch, he added, became a "forgotten social pastime."

At loose ends, with no prospect of work in sight, Jimmy seemed unable to orient himself. He drifted along, sleeping late, rarely leaving his hotel room before noon, and then not to go very far. He would sit for hours on the steps of the hotel barber shop, until Louis, the proprietor, chased him for blocking the entrance. Alec Wilder, who lived down the block at the Algonquin, recalled, "I don't know how many hundreds of times I'd come into the lobby and find Dean sprawled on the bellboys' bench." After Dean's death, the composer was unable to fathom the attention focused on the actor. "He was a kid," Wilder said, "with a kid's mind. He had no theories about politics. He liked comfort. He liked wine. He liked to tell jokes. He just hung around."

One weekend Dizzy came into town for a visit. *Has Anybody Seen My Gal?*, the movie Dean had done the summer before, had opened at the Mayfair Theater, and he, Dizzy, and Bast went to see it. When Dean came on screen, the three of them stood up and cheered. Dizzy convinced Jimmy to return to Ocean City with her, feeling the change might do him good. Dean went, but after several days of hanging around the sleepy resort he grew restless and was anxious to return to New York and try again for work.

He auditioned without success for a lead in a forthcoming television series, *Life With Father*, based on Clarence Day's best-selling book about life in turn-of-the-century America. He also tried to land the part of Curly in *Oklahoma!*, which Mike Todd was planning to bring to the screen. For his audition, Dean chose the song "I Could Write a Book." His enthusiasm, however, was stronger than his voice, and the Todd people passed him over. At the casting office Dean met a young actor named Paul Newman, whom he had seen at other auditions. "We were like the Bobbsey twins," Newman claimed. "Every place I went, he went." But, like Dean, Newman was not signed for the movie either.

In August, as summer reached its peak and the city turned into a drab desert of concrete, another opportunity shimmered on the horizon, like an oasis, and with that strange combination of luck and guile that had propelled him through life thus far, Dean was quick to reach for it.

He was offered a job as a deckhand aboard a yacht chartered by Lemuel Ayers, a friend of Rogers Brackett. A charming and talented Princeton graduate, Ayers was a well-known set designer and had coproduced Cole Porter's *Kiss Me Kate*. He was then preparing a new play for Broadway, *See the Jaguar*, by N. Richard Nash.

Although Ayers was part of the homosexual circle that swirled around Brackett and his friends, the producer lived with his wife and two children in an old Victorian house near Nyack, New York. Brackett and Dean sometimes spent weekends there, where Jimmy enjoyed himself entertaining Ayers's young children, Sarah and Jonathan.

Although Brackett had already suggested Dean for a part in Ayers's new play, the producer felt he lacked experience. But the job as deckhand was open.

Dean joined the crew and the sloop sailed for Martha's Vineyard. Aboard were Ayers, his wife, Shirley, and several guests. The trip lasted almost two weeks; the first day out the weather was bad and the sea turned rough. When the sloop reached New London, several people, including Alec Wilder, decided to get off and return by train. But Dean stayed, enjoying himself, quickly learning about lines and spars, sheets and shrouds—a farmboy turned deckhand. A young Gatsby in the making.

By the time the sloop returned to port, Ayers had been impressed enough by Dean to reconsider his earlier decision. He promised that when *See the Jaguar* was cast, Dean would be given a reading. Whether he got the part would depend on how well he did.

Before Dean left for the trip, he and Bast had decided to give up their hotel room. Apparently unconcerned about where he would live when he returned—after all, Bast noted, it "was a whole ten days off"—Dean left the problem of finding new quarters to his friend. Around this time, Jimmy briefly saw his old pal Jim Bellah. When Bellah asked what he was up to, Dean replied casually, "I've been a professional houseguest on Fire Island for the summer."

Bast found a temporary solution by moving in with an old girlfriend from UCLA, and Jimmy joined them. Shortly after Labor Day, however, the girl's lease was up and they were all forced to move again. Along with Dizzy, who had returned to the city and was now working as an usher at the Paris Theater, they found a small apartment at 13 West 89th Street in an old brownstone right off Central Park.

The new apartment proved something of an adventure at first. A brick street ran in front of the building, and every evening they could hear the sound of horses' hooves as the police cavalry returned to the stables down the block. The whole atmosphere, Bast wrote, suggested a quainter era, as though they were all back in the days of hansom cabs and horseless carriages, and Lillian Russell and Diamond Jim Brady were the talk of the town.

As the weeks rolled by, Dean kept in touch with Ayers's office, checking on the show's progress. Each time he called, though, Dean's disappointment grew: Plans were lagging; problems had arisen that no one had counted on.

From Brackett, Dean learned the producer was having

problems rounding up potential backers. *See the Jaguar* was Ayers's first dramatic venture, and investors were wary. Furthermore, there were difficulties casting the show's leads. One actor was waiting to see if he might be signed for Arthur Miller's *The Crucible* before committing himself to Ayers.

Privately, Brackett wondered if the show would get off the ground, but he urged Dean to be patient.

At this time, too, Dean's newest living arrangements were proving less than perfect. "After the novelty wore off," Bast wrote, "community living ceased to be an adventure and became a problem....If we weren't battling over the maze of bras, panties, and stockings that were making access to the bathroom impossible, we were haggling over the unwashed dishes...the selection of radio programs, etc., etc."

One evening after a skimpy meal of chili and beans, Dean announced he was going home to Indiana for a couple of weeks. He was tired of the delays on the show and wanted time to think about his future. He invited the others to go along. "We'll hitchhike out there," he told them. "It's only eight hundred miles." Dizzy accepted at once, and after some persuasion Bast decided to make the trip, too. Toni, their other roommate, promised to phone CBS every day and tell them Bast was sick.

With ten dollars to sustain them, and one battered suitcase, the three took a bus the next morning to the New Jersey Turnpike and started hitchhiking.

By nightfall they found themselves still in Pennsylvania, weary, hungry, and a long way from Fairmount. After having ice cream at a small roadside place, they got a ride with a man driving an old Nash Rambler. His name was Clyde McCullough and he was a catcher for the Pittsburgh Pirates. (McCullough later became a catching instructor for the New York Mets.) He was on his way to Des Moines, Iowa, to play a game with a team that was barnstorming across the country.

When they stopped for coffee, and McCullough discovered

his companions had hardly eaten, he insisted on buying them dinner.

They drove with him the rest of the way to Indiana, passing the cold night singing and telling stories, Jimmy and Dizzy huddled in the backseat to keep warm.

Just before dawn, they reached Fairmount and parted on the highway, all good friends.

On the farm, the three quickly entered into a new tempo and pace of life. They were up and about bright and early. Dean taught Dizzy how to shoot a rifle, using tin cans as targets. At the first opportunity, Dean got his old motorcycle out of the workshed and put on a daring exhibit of stunt riding. "I'll never sell it," he told Bast. "It's like a friend and brother to me. And friends are hard to find in the theater."

The Winslows were glad to have Jimmy home and made his two friends feel welcome. There were clean, warm beds and plenty to eat, and every night after supper everyone sat around talking.

"After all the years of seeing Jimmy alone and without a family," Bast commented, "it was a wonderful thing to watch him touch again the gentle roots of his early years. He was back in his element and he loved it."

"Someday when I make it," Dean vowed, "I'm going to see to it that they sell this place and move to a drier climate where Mom's arthritis won't bother her so much. Someday they're going to have the kind of life they deserve, without all the work and worry."

Dean revisited his high school and took Bast and Dizzy around town, showing them his boyhood haunts. He and Dizzy also went horseback riding, enjoying the Indiana countryside that had turned golden now in the early autumn. "I wish everybody could have been with us in Indiana," Dizzy later said, "and seen how good and simple Jimmy really was. I can remember his love for animals, how close he could get to them, and even the tender way he treated the soil around the farm."

After a week, there was an unexpected phone call from New York. It was Lemuel Ayers's office, telling Dean *Jaguar* was finally set to go into production and they wanted him to audition.

The next morning, Dean and his two friends were driven by Uncle Marcus to the main highway and started to thumb their way back.

All were silent and sorry to be leaving, but at least luck was with them: The first driver who stopped turned out to be going to New York. He was a wealthy oilman from Texas who suffered from ulcers. Every time they stopped for something to eat he would go outside and become violently ill. Finally Dean took the wheel, and as night fell, drove toward the city.

## 6

BACK IN NEW YORK, Jimmy prepared for his audition.

"He had a dream in the back of his mind all these months," Bast said, "and he was determined to make that dream come true."

On the night of his reading, dressed in a clean shirt he had borrowed from Bast and a pair of newly pressed slacks, Dean showed up at Ayers's office on West 57th. He was reading for the part of Wally Wilkins, a backward youth who finds himself at the mercy of a sadistic mountain community.

The part had been an extraordinarily difficult one to cast; over a hundred young actors had already been interviewed, including several in Hollywood and Chicago, and almost forty were invited to audition. "While we'd been considering some of the more promising ones," the director, Michael Gordon, remembers, "we'd found none who wholly satisfied us."

Gordon was alone in Ayers's office when Dean arrived. He later recalled: "Although Jimmy was strangely uncommunicative at our first encounter—totally unlike the average actor who's hardselling on a casting interview—I was instantly alerted to what seemed to me an exciting potential for the role. He was young enough to bring to the character the mixture of qualities the role called for. The question was, could he act?"

Gordon handed Dean a script and indicated one or two scenes he wanted him to read. Dean sat in the outer office studying the script for almost an hour. Then he and Gordon started going over the first scene. "It was only a matter of minutes until I saw that he was what I'd been searching and hoping for," Gordon said. "His impulses and criteria were right on the beam."

At twenty-one Dean was cast in his first Broadway play. He joined Arthur Kennedy and Constance Ford, who had already been selected for the two leads. Others in the cast included Roy Fant, Margaret Barker, George Tyne, David Clarke, Florence Sundstrom, and Cameron Prud'homme.

Rehearsals got under way on October 20, and Jimmy was soon right at home on Broadway, plastering his dressing room with bullfight posters and picture postcards of toreros he admired. "He claimed, among other things," the director remembers, "to have been a novillero in various bullrings south of the border, and I often saw him make daring passes and fariñas at onrushing taxicabs while crossing Broadway or Seventh Avenue."

For Dean, things went exceedingly well, and he got on smoothly with the others.

"He was a prince," Constance Ford said, "and the first time I saw him I knew it." Originally, Nash had wanted Maureen Stapleton for the lead, but the part went to Miss Ford, a television actress and former Conover model, after the other actress turned it down. At the playwright's suggestion Constance had dyed her hair brunette. When Dean wandered into her dressing room and saw her studying her new hair color, he told her: "It doesn't make you Maureen Stapleton." They became good friends.

Dean also fell under the influence of Arthur Kennedy, then a well-known stage actor. Dizzy Sheridan noticed that Jimmy began to walk and talk like his new mentor—a pattern he was later to follow with Brando. Alec Wilder thought that Kennedy's influence was "dreadful" since "to him nobody mattered except for the actor."

In the show, Dean played a young man who has spent most of his life in an icehouse, hidden away from the world by his half-demented mother. Upon her death, he emerges outside, only to be caged by a cruel storekeeper to whom his mother owed money. To get a feeling of what it was like to be penned in, Dean even locked himself in a closet and stayed there overnight.

Jimmy's identification with his role won over the director. Gordon later recalled: "In discussing the unique quality of an adolescent coming into a strange world (emerging from the womb, in a sense) for the first time, I mentioned to Dean the characteristic exploration of infants—touching, grasping, tasting. He made marvelously constructive use of this idea and it became a fascinating ingredient of his character. His intuitive impulses were beautiful and he had the courage as an actor to go with them. I never saw him do a job on TV or film that I felt surpassed the work he did in *See the Jaguar*."

As rehearsals progressed, however, it became clear the show was headed for difficulties. "There are some plays you remember as light," Margaret Barker later said. "This was all dark."

The play was undercapitalized, and to save money on an orchestra, Alec Wilder, who had been signed to write background music, was forced to write a score using only choral voices that could be put on tape.

Several actors thought the script was too ambiguous and that there was no rationale for the brutal behavior of the characters they portrayed. One actor, Tony Krabner, felt the play was a subtle warning against domestic Fascism, with the mountain hamlet representing a microcosm of the country as a whole. As things turned out, that interpretation proved as good as any.

The play opened out of town for a three-day run at the Parson's Theater in Hartford, Connecticut, before moving on to Philadelphia for a two-week engagement at the Forrest Theater. Actress Florence Sundstrom recalled that one night in Hartford the star of the show and his young protégé "got loaded on beer and landed" at her door at the old Taft Hotel.

The three "dished for a while about everything." Later Sundstrom said: "Too bad he died so young."

In Philadelphia notices in both the local papers were good and morale improved. Dean managed to enjoy himself. He and his understudy, Dane Knell, met some girls from another show who were staying at their hotel, and each night after the play they went on the town, staying out until the early morning hours.

On December 3, 1952, *See the Jaguar* opened at the Cort Theater on Broadway.

"We knew it was a flop opening night," Alec Wilder said. In the first act, the stereo equipment on which Wilder's music had been recorded broke down, and no one was able to fix it. In the second, the stage manager missed a prop cue and neglected to shoot a gun, marring a crucial scene. At the end of the act, Arthur Kennedy came off stage and said quietly, "Well, that's it."

At the traditional opening party at Sardi's, the cast and their friends waited for the morning papers and the critics' reactions.

Ayers and his wife tried their best to remain optimistic. The room was filled with people, and there was a great deal of noise and laughter. Actress Margaret Barker said afterward, "It was the nicest funeral I've ever been to."

Dean had invited Bast and Dizzy, and the three of them sat at a small table in the corner. Dean was ecstatic; his own dressing room had been jammed with well-wishers after the show and compliments about his performance had filled the air. Even Alec Wilder was impressed by Dean's performance. "He was like any other kid—until he went on stage," the composer recalled. "Then he was absolutely authoritative."

Every once in a while Dean excused himself and went off to mingle with the others. As Dizzy and Bast watched him bounce around the room, accepting congratulations or posing with his proud agent, they felt strangely depressed. They sensed the good times they had all had together were at an end, and that their old friend Jimmy was on his way, this time alone.

As expected, *See the Jaguar* received an unfavorable press. Brooks Atkinson, writing in the *New York Times,* called the production "a mess." Another critic claimed the play was "obscure," and in the *Daily News* John Chapman's review was headlined, "*See the Jaguar* Lovely to See and Hear, but It Makes No Sense."

Despite the hostile tone of the reviews, several critics singled Dean out for a brief word of praise. William Hawkins in the *World-Telegram & Sun* wrote, "James Dean is gently awkward as the ignorant boy." John Chapman called Dean's acting "very good," and Walter Kerr, the respected critic for the *Herald Tribune,* stated, "James Dean adds an extraordinary performance in an almost impossible role."

The play closed December 6 after five performances. But Dean had been noticed, and indeed he was on his way.

1953 began auspiciously. In January Dean appeared in a brief dramatic segment on the *Kate Smith Variety Show,* and also had a role on NBC's *T-Men in Action.* Dean played the son of a moonshiner whose mountain still is raided by Treasury agents.

Jane Deacy had left the Schurr office in August to start her own agency and had taken Dean with her. He soon became her hottest client. Job offers came in steadily, but Miss Deacy was careful to pick and choose: There were to be no more walk-ons, no more bits, no more playing bellhops.

In the beginning of February, Dean appeared on *You Are There,* a popular TV series that recreated historical events. The episode was "The Capture of Jesse James," and Dean played Bob Ford, the man who "shot poor Jesse in the back." The show aired on Jimmy's twenty-second birthday, and he considered it his "juiciest" role to date. "He loved the part," Sidney Lumet, the director, remembers, "loved handling guns, and used to practice 'quick draw' with all the pleasure of a child." Afterward, Dean would frequently tell friends it was his dream to make a "great western."

With the money he was earning, Dean permitted himself a few small luxuries. He bought a secondhand Leica camera and learned to operate it. He also purchased a glorious tome on bullfighting written in Spanish, José Cossio's *Los Toros*.

Since he could now afford a place of his own, Dean moved out of the apartment he had shared with the others and again took a room at the Iroquois Hotel. He and his old friends began to see less of each other, as they had expected. They all began to drift their separate ways. Dizzy was offered a job with a dancing troupe in the West Indies and moved to St. Thomas to live. Bast left for Hollywood, hoping to write scripts for a television show that was going into production. Before he left, Dean told him: "Remember...don't take any of their guff out there."

Dean began to spend a good deal of time alone now, studying, learning, seeking out new experiences. "An actor must have a cardinal interest in all things," he liked to say. "To interpret life you must study every aspect of it."

Music interested him, so he bought a recorder, an English flutelike instrument, and learned to play it, practicing in his room the simple tunes Alec Wilder would write.

He studied Roman history and dabbled in hypnosis. He tried the parachute jump at Coney Island and attended Christian Science lectures—all just for the experience.

He walked the city streets, stopping to talk to anyone who looked interesting, anyone he might learn from: shoeshine boys, newsstand operators, policemen. He became acquainted with short-order cooks, artists, and even a blind beggar named Moondog who dressed in flowing robes and made music using dried bones.

A cab driver, Arnie Langer, claimed: "Dean was always studying working people like me. When I finally saw him on TV, I realized he used me in some of his acting and he used other people I knew, too."

Actress Jean Alexander remembers once seeing Dean standing outside a restaurant for twenty minutes, just looking through the window at people while they ate; it was this detachment that led artist Ken Kendall to remember him as "the eternal spectator." Another actress, Arlene Sax, who met Dean at the Museum of Modern Art and whom he dated, later said: "When I was in a room with him, I always had the feeling I should open the window and say, 'Fly, Bird.'" Others were amazed by his intensity. One performer, Mildred Dunnock, who appeared with him on TV, recalls Jimmy "charging up the walls with energy."

It seemed anything interested him. "I think the prime reason for existence, for living in this world, is discovery," Jimmy later told writer Mike Connolly in an interview that was published posthumously [*Modern Screen*, December 1955]. There is a story that he once watched a parrot in a cage for a full hour, fascinated by the bird's behavior. There is another story that a month before his death Dean met a plumber and questioned the man incessantly, wanting to know everything about pipes and valves and the working of toilets.

Some who knew the actor claim this insatiable curiosity amounted to a foreknowledge that he did not have long to live, and that he wanted to utilize whatever time he had. Others feel differently. "He loved life so painfully," Arlene Sax believed, "he wanted to explore everything."

Sometimes Dean liked to boast, "Even if I live to be a hundred I'll never do all the things I want to do." But at other times he would sound fatalistic. "I'll never make it to the age of thirty," he confided to more than one friend.

In any event, Dean's life in New York was rich and full; new friends supplanted the old, his circle of acquaintances grew. There was very little lull between acting jobs, and now when he appeared on television, it was his name that frequently headed the cast list. He was not yet a star, but it was a portent of things to come.

A week after one such television show in which he had the

lead, Dean went into a department store to purchase some undergarments. The friend who was with him remembered that the clerk at the counter became deferential after recognizing Dean, but the actor was brusque and rude. "The last time I was in this store," he explained arrogantly, "nobody paid any attention to me. I was too small. All of a sudden I guess I've grown a few inches."

Alas, this also was a portent of things to come.

## 7

IN THE SPRING OF 1953 MGM offered to fly James Dean to Hollywood for a screen test. On the advice of Jane Deacy, he turned the offer down. Miss Deacy felt that her client was not yet ready for films, and that his TV career was going well enough so that he could wait.

Hollywood would beckon again, she assured him, and the next time their offer would have to be a better one.

In a single week in April, Dean had the lead in two separate television shows. In the first, he played a safecracker; two days later he appeared as a "reform school graduate" named Arbie Ferris on *T-Men in Action*. The show, entitled "Case of the Sawed-off Shot Gun," was sandwiched in between *Amos & Andy* and a Yankee-Senators baseball game. Another young actor, named Ben Gazzara, was also in the cast.

The program notes state simply: "Arbie learned the hard way, almost too late, that crime does not pay."

But Dean was learning crime did pay—or playing criminals did, anyway. Usually he commanded between two and three hundred dollars for a show, which was not bad, considering it only involved four or five days' work, including rehearsals.

Invariably, Dean played offbeat roles. In *Keep Our Honor Bright* Jimmy was a college student who masterminded a cheating scandal; the show appeared opposite *Dragnet,* the popular cops and robbers drama that starred Jack Webb as the no-nonsense Sergeant Friday. In *A Long Time Till Dawn,* Dean played a hot-tempered youth in trouble with the law. The latter show was aired in November 1953. The opening scene is set in a diner, and Dean appears hunched over a table, mumbling his lines and twirling a cigarette, his trademark mannerisms that later became famous.

As Dean had almost no head for money, Jane Deacy wisely held on to all his earnings, and he lived off an allowance she gave him. Whenever he wanted something extra, he had to ask her. Reluctantly, she permitted him to have a motorcycle, and Dean bought an Indian 550, a sleek machine he dashed around the city on, often with a pretty girl seated behind him.

He now moved out of his hotel, too, first subletting an apartment on West 56th Street from an airline pilot, and then taking a small flat of his own on the top floor of a brownstone at 19 West 68th Street. Right off Central Park, the building was in a neighborhood Dean could rightly call his old one.

The apartment soon became a gathering place for other young actors. "The same people were always there," someone said, "and nobody ever wanted to go home." The regulars included Marty Landau, a friend from Dean's days on *Beat the Clock,* and Bill Gunn, a young Negro who introduced Dean to the bongo drums. (Actor Dean Knell claimed that after Dean's death, Gunn went to his apartment and removed some poems that might have proved embarrassing to his friend. If so, the poems have disappeared.)

But Dean himself moved in many different worlds and various milieus; he seldom introduced his friends to each other and each one knew him as something different. "He had a vital gift for bringing people into their own focus," said Rusty Slocum. "When you were with Jimmy, he could make you feel like you were the one person in his life." Slocum was an eighteen-year-old would-be actor who hung around with Dean and was part of his circle. It was a crowd he later cryptically, or maybe not so cryptically, described as "Jimmy's little girlfriends and boyfriends."

Anyway, women moved in and out of Dean's life in rapid

succession; friends soon lost count of them. He would meet a girl at Walgreen's or Cromwell's Rockefeller Center drugstore in the morning, and by the evening she would be replaced by someone else.

Some lingered longer. He went out with Betsy Palmer, with whom he appeared on a television show, and spent a good deal of time with Arlene Sax. "He could make a moment," Arlene said. "Just walking down the street with him was like an adventure."

Betsy thought Dean was basically disinterested in the sex act. But Arlene has different recollections: "He was an Aquarius and I'm an Aries," she said, "and the two of us really got it on together."

Once, Arlene remembers, they got carried away and were surprised in the middle of lovemaking by a friend who had gone out to buy groceries. When Dean was dating Arlene, she was still in high school—a junior. Around the same time, he was seeing a wealthy debutante, too.

Intellectually this was also an exciting time for Jimmy. He read Kafka and T. E. Lawrence, Hemingway's *Death in the Afternoon*, and even *I Go Pogo*. He hung out in Greenwich Village at places like Minetta's and the San Remo, and went to film showings at art houses, seeing the movies of Gérard Philipe and Harry Baur. "Anyone who hasn't seen Harry Baur doesn't know what movie art can be," Dean said of the French actor who had appeared in the French-language version of *Crime and Punishment*. Now that Jimmy had some money, the city was truly his. He admired the Picassos at the Museum of Modern Art and dined at the Russian Tea Room. Sometimes he would hop in a cab and tell the driver to just throw down the meter and ride.

But Dean never lost track of his primary purpose—to grow as an actor. "His appetite for life was enormous," the director Herman Shumlin remarked, "but acting was his place in this world."

As a change from the criminals he was playing on television, Dean sought other roles. Jane Bowles wanted him for the lead in her play *In the Summer House,* but producer Oliver Smith thought he wasn't right for the part. Through Frank Corsaro, however, Dean landed a small part in an off-Broadway production of *The Scarecrow,* a play that was based on a short story by Nathaniel Hawthorne. Jimmy played a ghost. The show opened at the Theater De Lys June 16, 1953, for a limited two-week engagement, and Dean appeared along with Eli Wallach, William Redfield, and Patricia Neal.

Corsaro was a Yale graduate who became known for his innovative opera productions. He found Dean "a strong personality cloaked under the mask of a young fawn." Corsaro later said of his friend: "No matter what other mediums he worked in, Dean would have eventually returned to the stage. He needed the applause, the sympathy with an audience. How do you think his memory has survived all these years, if he hadn't had that ability to communicate with people?"

At Corsaro's suggestion, Dean did something he swore he would never do: He made peace with Lee Strasberg and returned to the Actors Studio.

The peace was never more than an uneasy one. "Jimmy was always talking about the Studio," remembers Claire Heller. "One minute he'd say how terrific it was. Then the next minute he'd tell you the whole thing was a lot of crap. He was very changeable." His opinion of Strasberg also varied; the director would be a "genius" or a "phony" depending on Jimmy's mood.

Strasberg took note of the young actor and his work. He believed that Dean had "a sense of not caring what happened to him" and that he radiated "nervousness, doubts, and concern." But to the Studio's director this "ferment" was part of the creative process since "an actor and his instrument cannot be separate."

Dean appeared as the cadet Starkson in the original Studio production of *End As a Man,* and played Pierrot in a production of Edna St. Vincent Millay's *Aria Da Capo.* Director Fred Stewart wanted to do the play in public, but Miss Millay's sister

Norma, her literary executrix, considered the production too avant-garde.

Dean also did a scene from Chekov's *The Sea Gull* with Joseph Anthony, who later directed *The Rainmaker* on Broadway. Dean played Treplev, and, according to Anthony, "Dean totally identified with the character, a fellow wanting to be a writer, on the outs with society, and in trouble with his family." To think himself into the role, Dean told Anthony he pretended the redoubtable Stella Adler was his mother. Strasberg said afterward he thought the scene was "lovely."

As Dean's reputation as an actor grew, so did his reputation as a personality. Within New York acting circles he was now known as something of a character, an eccentric. Ever since his school days in Fairmount, Dean had stood out from the others, and now in the most diverse city in the world he continued to do so. It was no small feat.

Sometimes he might drop by a friend's apartment, say hello, take some food from the refrigerator, eat, and then depart without saying another word. Peanut butter and pickles were a favorite dish. He brought his drums to his friend Jerry Lucce's restaurant and played them to the annoyance of other diners.

At photographer Roy Schatt's apartment, Dean once took a chair and sat in the street on it, disregarding the traffic. Another time, Schatt recalls, Dean somehow wound up standing in the nude on the sidewalk. "He was a mess," Schatt said. Their friendship ended in a quarrel when Dean refused to loan the struggling photographer money for a camera. After Dean's death, Schatt was always available for an interview. Sometimes his comments were malicious—and untrue, e.g., that Dean did not like Negroes. However unjustified, perhaps Jimmy's arrogance in success invited such revenge.

Dean would go days without shaving and carried around a revolver with one bullet in it. He bought a porkpie hat and wore it indoors and out until he tired of it. One friend remembers waiting for Dean in a hotel lobby and having him show up dressed in a dyed-black trenchcoat, wearing a Swedish candle ring on his head. He had just bought the ornament in a thrift shop, he explained.

This was in an era when even actors were expected to dress conventionally. "You were supposed to respect your craft," Richard Grayson explains. "If you showed up at a casting office without a jacket and tie they might not let you audition."

But Jimmy dressed as he pleased and acted as he pleased. During a rehearsal for a *Studio One* drama entitled "Sentence of Death," director Matt Harlib was startled to find Dean in a corner standing on his head. He found it relaxing, the actor said.

At an interview with casting agent Marion Daugherty, Dean went to sleep and had to be revived with coffee. His chronic lateness drove directors and fellow actors crazy. Once he missed a dress rehearsal entirely; he was sitting alone in a coffee shop and forgot about it. Another time, kidding around at an audition, he knocked a female producer's hat off. "He was a crazy boy," she later remembered.

After a meeting with Dean, producer Lawrence Langner drew a caricature of him and hung it on his office wall. He labeled it "a commentary on the sad state of the modern actor." The drawing looks remarkably like one of Saint-Exupéry's illustrations for *The Little Prince*, Dean's favorite book, the story of the little man "who laughs, who has golden hair, and who refuses to answer questions."

Still, Dean continued to work, and directors continued to seek his services. "If you knew your job," claims John Peyser, "Jimmy respected you and gave no trouble. It was a pleasure to direct him."

Pointing Dean out to a friend, director Homer Fickett said, "To look at him you wouldn't think he's playing with a full deck, but he's really quite sharp." One director, Bob Simon, even found Jimmy "fun to work with."

Paul Huber remembered that, one night at the Lambs

Club, another actor began a conversation about Dean by saying, "That little son of a bitch."

Such was Dean's inventiveness that he would seldom do a scene twice in the same way. He was forever experimenting, searching for ways to get deeper inside a role or make a scene come alive. Even decades later, actors would recall touches Jimmy brought to his roles. Jay Barney remembered that on *Studio One* Dean played a condemned man. During an interview with the prison chaplain, Dean wanted to giggle "to show a lack of contact with reality," but the director had him play the part straight.

In one television show in which Dean played a young man hospitalized after a suicide attempt, he suggested he play with a toy while lying in the hospital bed. "It was a lovely piece of business," writer George Roy Hill remembers, "and just right for a scene that might have otherwise been somewhat on the maudlin side." Dean liked the effect so well that he later employed it again: The movie *Rebel Without a Cause* opens with Dean lying intoxicated on the sidewalk, playing with a toy monkey—the innocent youth in a cold, hard world.

But all that was still in the future; television was Dean's present métier and his career moved along without so much as the slightest setback.

The early 1950s was an exciting time in television; some would later regard it as the medium's Golden Age. Original dramas filled the airwaves, shows like *Studio One, Kraft Television Theatre,* and *Armstrong Circle Theater* enjoyed great popularity.

Dean appeared on all of them, working with performers like Dorothy Gish, Jessica Tandy, and Ed Begley; doing scripts by promising new writers like Hill and Rod Serling.

And Dean's reputation continued to grow.

In August 1953, Producer Franklin Heller cast him in a drama, *Death Is My Neighbor,* with Walter Hampden, the distinguished Shakespearean actor and president of the Players Club.

Heller admired Hampden and regarded him as "one of the fine gentlemen of the theater." Although he had known the actor for many years, he had never called him anything but Mr. Hampden. He was therefore shocked "when Jimmy, upon being introduced to him, instantly addressed him as Walter." When Heller took the young actor aside and chided him for his familiarity, Dean told him that he didn't understand "why everyone was making such a fuss over 'some old cat.'" Then, Dean abruptly walked out of the studio "without saying a word." Always unpredictable, he reappeared the next day and got on with rehearsal as though nothing had happened.

Dean quickly learned why Hampden was treated with respect, even veneration, by those who recognized a true pro. Director John Peyser recalled that after the cast had gone over the script, he called Dean and Hampden together to block the first scene. It was a highly dramatic one in which Jimmy told the old man of his misdeeds, and the old man felt pity.

Peyser recalled that as Hampden began speaking his lines, tears welled up in the old man's eyes. His voice sounded choked and everyone appeared deeply moved. Then, abruptly, Hampden stopped and turned to the director. In a clear voice, he asked, "Is that what you want, Mr. Peyser?" Peyser replied, "Yes, thank you, Mr. Hampden." Dean seemed stunned by the old actor's technique; his jaw dropped and he gazed at Hampden in amazement. Peyser recalled afterward that "from then on, during rehearsals, Mr. Hampden could not start to sit down unless Jimmy was there placing a chair for him."

The show aired on October 6, 1953. Jimmy played a disturbed youth who plans the murder of a young girl who had spurned his advances. Betsy Palmer played the girl, whose life is saved when the police unravel her admirer's plot.

"A comparative newcomer, James Dean, stole the spotlight," *Variety* wrote, "delivering a magnetic performance that brought a routine meller [slang for melodrama] alive. He's got quite a future ahead of him."

Hampden told the producer: "That young man put me on

my toes and I'll wager he'll have the same effect on any other actor he works with, and though I won't live to see it, someday he'll be listed on the rostrum of truly great thespians."

At the time he said this, Hampden was in his seventies and had little more than a year to live; Dean had slightly less than two.

## 8

IN 1954 JAMES DEAN returned to Broadway.

Terese Hayden, a talent scout who had seen Dean in *See the Jaguar* and had been closely following his work on television, recommended him to Herman Shumlin the director. Shumlin was a well-regarded figure who previously had directed Lillian Hellman's *Little Foxes* on Broadway; he was then casting *The Immoralist*, a dramatization of André Gide's early autobiographical novel about homosexuality.

At their first meeting, Dean arrived at the director's 48th Street office on his motorcycle, wearing hip-length boots, a fringed jacket, and a huge hat. Shumlin found him "a startling sight," but he was impressed enough by Dean's audition to ask him to read again for the show's authors, Ruth and Augustus Goetz, and the producer, Billy Rose.

Dean did, and was cast as the blackmailing Arab, Bachir, in the play. Jimmy visited local rug stores to study Middle Eastern accents and, to absorb himself in the role, listened to Arab music with his friend and understudy Bill Gunn (who later became a noted playwright).

The cast was small, numbering only eight actors. Louis Jourdan played a young French archaeologist tormented by guilt over his homosexuality. Geraldine Page was his wife, who naively attributes the barrenness of their relationship to a severe fever her husband contracts on their honeymoon in Africa.

Rehearsals got under way on December 18 at the old Ziegfeld building on Sixth Avenue where Rose had his offices. Almost at once, Dean fell under Shumlin's spell, adopting him as a father figure. Shumlin, in turn, found the young actor a "remarkable and unusual personality whose endless variety in experimenting with his role fascinated me—up to a point. Then I decided I wanted him to stop and settle on one interpretation, which he did to my satisfaction."

But all was not entirely well. Jimmy had a habit of disappearing when he was on call. This delayed rehearsals while other cast members tried to locate him. Once, he annoyed the stage manager by playing tic-tac-toe on the scenery. There were also murmurs from other actors that Shumlin was allowing Dean far too much freedom on stage. Paul Huber, a veteran actor who had appeared in John Barrymore's Broadway production of *Hamlet*, claims, "Dean played every scene for himself. He tried to make improvisation of the whole damn play."

Adelaide Klein, who had several scenes opposite Dean, remembers simply, "Jimmy was a tough kid to work with." Another actor, Salem Ludwig, stopped speaking to Dean.

Relations did not improve any when Dean began storing his motorcycle in the cramped backstage area, and his fellow actors were forced to glide around it.

Adding to the director's problems, the Goetzes were unhappy with his treatment of their script and they urged Rose to intervene.

Initially, the dynamic little impresario had stayed aloof from the production, explaining, "I really don't know from fairies." But as rehearsals continued to go downhill, he stepped in and fired Shumlin. "I like the cast, Herman," Rose is supposed to have said, "but I'm afraid I miscast the director."

A courtly and soft-spoken man, Shumlin bowed out graciously and was replaced by Daniel Mann, who had previously directed *The Rose Tattoo* on Broadway. Mann was the opposite of Shumlin: a tough, no-nonsense guy who had grown up in Brooklyn and had served as a tank officer in the Second World

War. He was ready for any contingency and was certainly a match for young Mr. Dean. The new director joined the company shortly before it left for its January tryout in Philadelphia.

The situation Mann inherited was precarious, and in Philadelphia he and the others worked around the clock to prepare for the opening.

The script was revised and a new ending written. At a cost of some nineteen thousand dollars, new sets were also ordered after Mrs. Goetz claimed the original scenery had left her "heartbroken."

In the rewriting, Dean's part was cut, and with his mentor Shumlin gone, he now seemed to lose all interest in the production—and all sense of restraint. He clashed with the producer; he was late on cues. "There are other people on stage," the director would remind him. "Cut that shit out." There were moments when Dean went dead on the part completely. When Mrs. Goetz reprimanded him after one rehearsal, Dean told her, "I think I did all right."

As Dean had a run-of-the-play contract, Rose was reluctant to fire him, since he would have to pay him his salary of three hundred dollars a week until the play closed.

Then, after one encounter with Mann in which the director rebuked him sharply, Dean walked out of the rehearsal hall and his place was taken by his understudy. As he left, Jimmy murmured, "Nobody can push me around." It was assumed that Dean would be automatically fired, as Equity rules permitted, but when he returned to the theater an hour later, David J. Stewart, the Equity representative, miraculously smoothed things over, and Dean rejoined the cast.

"Dean was an actor driven by strange impulses," Mann remembered. "He was compulsive, difficult to reach, and totally uncooperative. In *The Immoralist* he was a destructive force. And yet at the same time he had flashes of real brilliance."

Others felt this brilliance, too. "He moved like a snake,"

Abe Feder said. "You could literally feel the sensuality pouring over the stage."

Even so, the quality of Dean's work continued to vary. Opening night in Philadelphia he was at his best, but the next night his performance was so listless that Rose stormed backstage afterward and told him, "Don't you ever do that to me again."

The critics, however, had only been there opening night, and notices were good. The reviewer for the *Evening Bulletin* praised the production for its "restraint" and "sensitivity" and called the cast "extraordinary." Jourdan, Page, and Dean all received glowing reviews. "There is an excellent performance by James Dean as an insinuating Arab houseboy," the *Bulletin's* critic wrote, and added, "He was the caged lad in *See the Jaguar* last year, you may recall."

After three weeks in Philadelphia, the play returned to New York for a week of paid previews at the Royale Theater before officially opening.

At one preview, an old friend of the Goetzes named Paul Osborn saw the play and was particularly impressed by Dean.

Osborn, a playwright *(On Borrowed Time)* and screenwriter *(Portrait of Jennie)*, was at work on a movie treatment of John Steinbeck's *East of Eden*. The next day he phoned the man who was to direct the picture and told him about this young actor he had seen.

The man Osborn called was Elia Kazan.

One of the best-known directors in America, Kazan was then under exclusive contract to Warner Brothers to make a picture a year, and the studio had given him virtual carte blanche to initiate and develop his own projects.

Kazan had started out as an actor with the Group Theater in the 1930s and had appeared in several Clifford Odets plays, but later turned to directing. In 1947 he had created a sensation on Broadway with his staging of Tennessee Williams's *A Streetcar Named Desire* and had helped make an overnight star of Marlon Brando.

Since then, Kazan had been alternating between Broadway and Hollywood, where he had made such films as *Man on a Tightrope, Viva Zapata!,* and *On the Waterfront,* the last of which would soon bring him his second Academy Award as Best Director.

Dean's name was not new to Kazan; the director had seen and been impressed with the young actor's audition at the Actors Studio. He had also seen Dean on television, and at one point had even considered him for the Broadway lead in *Tea and Sympathy,* playing a prep school student whose classmates falsely accuse him of homosexuality. But the role went instead to John Kerr, a Harvard graduate whose clean-cut looks better suited him to play the upper-class youngster.

Osborn's tip once again aroused Kazan's sharp casting instincts, and he now thought Dean might be just right for the part of Cal Trask, the difficult and troublesome son in the Steinbeck story.

After seeing Dean on stage, Kazan went around to talk to him. "I just got to know the guy," Kazan later said. "I hung around with him…and rode around on his motorcycle. I'd already made up my mind he was going to play it. I realized it wasn't a matter of could he or couldn't he; he was it."

To writer Joe Hyams, Kazan elaborated further: "I chose Jimmy because he *was* Cal Trask. There was no point in attempting to cast it nicer or bigger….He had a grudge against all fathers. He was vengeful; he had a sense of aloneness and of being persecuted. And he was suspicious. In addition, he was tremendously talented."

Kazan sent Dean to meet John Steinbeck, who was then living in New York. The author found Dean "a snotty kid," and told Kazan so, but agreed he was right for the part.

As expected, *The Immoralist* opened on Broadway to solid critical acclaim. The reviews in both the *Times* and the *Herald Tribune* were favorable. "It would be hard to find serious fault with the production," wrote the *Herald Tribune*'s Walter Kerr. Only the critic for the New York *Journal-American,* a Hearst publication, struck a completely sour note, calling the play's theme "fare for a small and specialized audience."

Dean attracted the most attention he had to date. Reviewers for five major daily papers praised his performance. The *Times*'s Brooks Atkinson claimed Dean brought "insidious charm" to the role, and even Richard Watts of the *New York Post*, whose feelings about the play were mixed, was complimentary toward Dean.

On opening night, however, as a way of getting even with Rose, Dean gave notice he was leaving the play. He took delight in posting the announcement backstage on a bulletin board. During the preceding weeks the producer had often shouted at Dean during their arguments, "This is Rose speaking." But now the actor had the last word; across the top of the paper he scrawled: "This is Dean speaking." Rose failed to see the humor. In his Runyonesque manner, he afterward referred to Dean as "a punk" and "goddamn ingrate."

Jimmy remained with the play the required two weeks, and left the cast on February 20. Although he was out of work, he must surely have been the happiest unemployed actor in New York. Elia Kazan and agent Jane Deacy were busy ironing out his Hollywood contract, and, in the meantime, he was free to do as he liked.

His aunt and uncle had come to New York to see *The Immoralist*, and Jimmy now squired them around town, proudly introducing them to his friends as "my folks from Indiana."

Never able to remain idle very long, Dean was soon involved in an informal production of Sophocles' *Women of Trachis* at the New School for Social Research. The play was a new translation by Ezra Pound and had appeared in the winter *Hudson Review*. (Pound had translated the work at St. Elizabeth's mental hospital, where he was incarcerated for allegedly having committed treason during World War II.) Eli Wallach and Joseph Sullivan were also in the cast, and Howard Sackler, later author of *The Great White Hope*, directed. The production was repeated at the uptown YMHA.

As ever, directors either loved or hated Dean; Sackler was no exception. He remembers fondly: "Dean was a pleasure to work with, and he had a superb instinct for 'classical' acting—elevation without inflation. His death cost us not only a movie star, but also an Orestes, a Hamlet, a Peer Gynt—that is, an actor who could really act."

Then, in March, just before Dean's movie contract was finalized, Warner Brothers began to question the wisdom of using an unknown actor in such a major role. "To them," Kazan said, "it was like taking a horse from a horse and carriage and putting him in the Belmont Stakes."

To set the studio at ease, Kazan shot a brief screen test at the Gjon Mili studio in which Dean played a scene opposite costar Julie Harris.

After Warners saw the test there were no further protests. Dark horse or not, the feeling at the studio was that Elia Kazan was clearly getting set to ride home another winner.

*9*

JAMES DEAN'S ARRIVAL in Hollywood in the spring of 1954 was unobtrusive.

Elia Kazan had already made clear to the studio that he wanted no buildup for the young actor, and his presence went totally unnoticed by the Hollywood press.

Dean quickly found a place to live, sharing a small fifty-dollar-a-month apartment with Dick Davalos, another young actor who was in the movie. The apartment was above a drugstore in Burbank, right across the street from Warner Brothers.

Dean's salary for the picture was ten thousand dollars, and with the money the studio advanced him he bought a beautiful palomino horse, which he named Cisco and boarded at a stable in nearby Griffith Park.

As Jane Deacy did not have a West Coast office, she had arranged for the Famous Artists Agency to look after her client. The office assigned this task to Dick Clayton, one of its younger agents; the choice proved to be a wise one. Handsome and easygoing, Clayton was a former actor who had appeared in *High Sierra* and *The Wagons Roll at Night*. He knew his way around the film colony, and he knew how to handle actors. Several days after their first meeting, Clayton arranged for Dean to buy a small sports car, an MG, and shortly thereafter Dean could be seen whizzing around town, usually accompanied by an attractive ingenue whose phone number the agent had thoughtfully provided.

Shooting for *East of Eden* began on schedule in the middle of May. Kazan and his scenarist had decided beforehand to film only the last quarter of the book, dealing with the relationship of the two Trask brothers, Cal and Aron (Cain and Abel), and their father, Adam. "I didn't read the novel," Dean later told reporter Howard Thompson. "The way I work, I'd much rather justify myself with the adaptation rather than the source."

The film is set in rural California, as America is poised to enter the First World War. Raymond Massey played the senior Trask, a stern and pious man who looks to the Scriptures for guidance. Jo Van Fleet played the wife who had deserted him and the boys years before. She is hard and cynical—a madam who runs a thriving whorehouse and thinks she spots in her younger son a budding entrepreneur. Julie Harris played Abra, a young girl in love with both the Trask sons.

In the movie, Dean attempts to raise money for his father by growing crops to feed the army; instead of showing gratitude, the old man is aghast at his son's war profiteering. Dean's attempt at finding love sours—a familiar theme in his life and films. On another level, the movie symbolizes the destruction of the old morality by atavistic capitalism.

The rest of the fine company Kazan had assembled included Albert Dekker, Harold Gordon, Barbara Baxley, Burl Ives, and Lon Chapman. Richard Davalos, another Kazan discovery, who only months before had been working as a movie usher, was cast as Aron, the more gentle Trask son, and the favorite of his father.

Warner Brothers was determined to spare no expense in mounting the production. A replica of the town of Salinas, the setting for the story, was carefully constructed on the studio lot; the producer fired off memos having his staff check on the smallest details: "What was the World War I duffel bag like?"

"Did they use flashbulbs or powder in 1917?" Even the town stores were stocked with actual merchandise.

From the very start, Kazan worked closely with Dean. The director knew that the young actor, who showed up on the set "blue and tense and bewildered," required his personal attention. "Jimmy was very naked, very easily hurt," Kazan explained. "First I'd work with him to build up his confidence. Then I'd give him a small shove in the right direction."

The two would often go into long huddles discussing a scene, and to loosen Dean up, Kazan would sometimes spar with him until the actor was ready to work. When a take still proved difficult, Kazan resorted to other means. As he later told writer Glenn O'Brien, "One time we spent all afternoon on a scene and he couldn't do it, so I got him loaded on red wine that night. He couldn't drink a lot because he was sort of unstable and liquor would affect him, but I gave him two glasses of wine and he did the scene great."

Much as been printed about Kazan's tricks in coaxing Dean's memorable performance. But according to Lon Chapman, a fellow Studio member, Dean resented the director's use of gimmicks "and complained it wasn't acting."

"Working with Jimmy Dean and Raymond Massey was wonderful," Julie Harris later said. "Jimmy was very gifted. There was nothing he couldn't do. He was terribly interesting. He enjoyed being naughty—like Tom Sawyer."

Massey, an Oxford-educated actor, didn't share this appreciation. "He simply couldn't stand the sight of the kid," Kazan later remembered. "You never know what he's going to say or do," Massey would complain to the director. "Make him read the lines the way they're written." But Kazan seized on this antagonism to sharpen the on-screen tension between the staid father and his rebellious son. During one scene in which Adam Trask sternly reads the Bible to his sons, Kazan had Dean whisper obscenities under his breath to heighten Raymond Massey's anger. It worked very nicely.

Kazan's own feelings toward Dean were mixed, and this inconsistency was reflected in later interviews. On one occasion, he explained: "Jimmy wasn't easy because it was all new to him. He was like an animal might be. Fretful or uncertain. But with affection and understanding and patience he got awfully good. God, he gave everything he had. There wasn't anything he held back. Only at the very, very end—the last few days when you felt that a star was going to be born, and everybody smelled it, all the publicity people began to hang around him— then he began to spoil, I thought, a little bit. By the next film I thought something in his character was spoiling."

However, in a less generous mood he told the *London Daily Express:* "Jimmy was a pretty difficult and at most times a thoroughly impossible character. He got on badly with his fellow actors and the crew who made the film.

"The girl who really helped him through *East of Eden* was Julie Harris. She was like a saint with him, even though when she did a good scene he would try to ruin it.

"His great love was himself and he spent a good deal of his time off the set taking pictures of himself with a camera."

Early in June the cast went on location for several weeks near the town of Spreckels, in the Salinas Valley. Here Kazan filmed the sequences involving Adam Trask's ill-fated lettuce refrigeration project and Cal's bean crop venture. Other location scenes were taken at the picturesque town of Mendocino on the coast north of San Francisco.

Dean had recently bought a Triumph T–110 motorcycle and planned to ride to Spreckels on it, but Kazan quickly vetoed the idea. "Nothing doing, Jimmy," the director told him. "I can't take a chance that you'll spill." Since Dean was known as a daredevil rider, Kazan's caution was undoubtedly wise. "You expect to take a fall once a year," Jimmy told one reporter. "If he had to kill himself," Kazan said later, "I'd rather not have him do it during my movie."

When the cast returned from location, Dean decided to move out of his apartment and live in his studio dressing room, a luxurious two-room suite once used by such stars as Bette Davis and Errol Flynn. Kazan, who lived in the adjoining dressing room, encouraged the move. "I kept my eye on him night and day," he said, "so we'd be sure to get through the goddamn picture."

One afternoon during a break in filming, Dean wandered over to an adjacent set to visit two friends, Paul Newman and Joseph Wiseman, who were making a picture called *The Silver Chalice*. They introduced him to another member of the cast, a lovely Italian-born actress named Pier Angeli.

At twenty-one, Anna Maria Pierangeli was very special. She had green eyes, delicate, almost doelike features, and light brown hair. "She's out of this world," Dean once said. The daughter of an engineer, Pier had been an art student in Rome before being discovered by Vittorio De Sica and becoming an actress. She had first come to Hollywood to play an Italian war bride in the movie *Teresa*, and was now living in Brentwood with her mother and two sisters, one of whom, Marisa Pavan, Pier's twin, was also an actress.

Soon Pier and James Dean were visiting each other's sets daily and sharing quiet lunches in a corner of the studio commissary. Their whispering and handholding became the talk of the studio, and items about the budding romance began to appear in various gossip columns. "James Dean has the lead in *East of Eden* and you'll be hearing of him soon," columnist Sidney Skolsky wrote, on June 29, 1954. "Pier Angeli, who isn't in the movie, has discovered him already."

The items quickly came to the attention of Pier's mother, a strict, old-fashioned woman who did not consider Dean, a non-Catholic, a suitable boyfriend for her daughter. But despite Mrs. Pierangeli's objections, the couple continued to see each other. They went for quiet early-morning horseback rides along a Hollywood trail, and Dean brought Pier to a party at Elia Kazan's. Dean took his drums along and he and Pier played them together.

Then, one evening, Dean brought Pier home long after her

curfew. When Mrs. Pierangeli reprimanded him, Jimmy told her she was "too strict" with Pier. After that, Mrs. Pierangeli forbade her daughter to see Dean again, and even tried to get the studio to keep the young couple apart; but when Pier threatened to leave home, her mother relented and the romance continued.

On Pier's twenty-second birthday she and Dean spent the day at Griffith Park washing and currying Dean's horse, Cisco.

"Pier is a rare girl," Dean told a friend. "I respect her. Unlike most Hollywood girls, she's real and genuine."

To his old friend Bill Bast, he explained: "I can talk to her. She understands."

"Jimmy is different," Pier was quoted as saying. "He loves music. He loves it from the heart the way I do. We have so much to talk about. It's wonderful to have such understanding."

Pier's influence had a strong effect on Dean. He became neater in his habits and even started to drive more carefully, as Pier disapproved of his speeding. To show his affection, he showered her with presents and proudly took her home to meet his father and stepmother. "The young lion," a writer quipped, "was being tamed by love."

This sudden change in Dean both surprised and amused his friends. Actress Connie Ford recalled her amazement at seeing Dean at a dinner party wearing a navy blue suit and a smart Italian knit tie. It was the first time the actress had ever seen him with his hair combed. Pier sat next to him, looking radiant in a white chiffon dress.

On another occasion Dean even donned a tuxedo and escorted Pier to the premiere of *A Star Is Born*, a gala event held at the Pantages Theater and attended by such personalities as Marlene Dietrich and Clark Gable. Studios then arranged for their young male stars to attend premieres with attractive ingenues. Often it was a publicity ploy to project a virile image. Paramount had once forced young Monty Clift to suffer through the ritual. But dodging flashbulbs and autographs hounds with Pier was no chore for Jimmy.

As the couple grew closer, inevitably, rumors of marriage began to circulate. "Do you think eventually you kids will get married?" a reporter boldly asked Dean. "You mean me and Miss Pizza?" he replied evasively. "Who knows?"

Although he and Pier had often talked of marriage, Dean was torn by indecision. He told Joe Hyams that he was considering becoming a Catholic so he and Pier could marry. But he confided to another friend that he feared being tied down and felt he was not ready. "I wouldn't marry her unless I could take care of her properly," he admitted. "And I don't think I'm emotionally stable enough to do so right now."

But for Pier the issue seemed simpler. "She thought if he really loved her, he would marry her," a friend said. The subject became a sore point between them, and for the first time there were quarrels and recriminations.

Late in August Dean completed his work on *East of Eden* and went to New York to do a TV show, "Run Like a Thief," on NBC's *Philco Playhouse*. The program aired on September 5, 1954, and Jimmy played a young man who is suspected of robbery. Both Pier and the question of marriage were very much on his mind. Gusti Huber, who was in the cast, remembers Dean spoke of Pier constantly, and once during a break in rehearsal ran to Best & Co. to buy her a present.

Miss Huber was impressed by the young actor's energy and range of interests. During rehearsals, he talked to her about Hugo Wolf, the Austrian composer; Frank Sinatra; *Charlotte's Web* by E. B. White; and Bob and Ray, two radio comedians whose ad-libbing style he admired. She remembered warning Jimmy, "You can't improvise until air time and then do a show." This undoubtedly fell on deaf ears.

Dean talked over his dilemma about marriage with Jane Deacy, his agent, and she advised him to wait until he was better established. From Miss Deacy's standpoint this no doubt was sound advice. She knew Dean's impulsive nature and had often cautioned him before; just a few months earlier he had even come to her wanting to change his name to Marcus Dean, but she had calmly talked him out of it.

Jimmy was away from Los Angeles only two weeks, but when he returned he sensed something had changed in his relationship with Pier.

They still saw each other, but now Pier appeared in public with other men, too. Once again, columnists were treated to a field day, this time chronicling the romance's demise. "The romance of James Dean and Pier Angeli is colder than ice," Louella Parsons informed her readers.

Then, in October, Pier suddenly announced her engagement to singer Vic Damone, whom she had first met while making a picture in Germany three years before, and whom she had recently been dating. Pier's decision surprised her family. Years later, her mother recalled how her daughter had waltzed into their living room one day and announced, "I'm going to marry Vic Damone."

Dean was absolutely stunned. "Oh, no, please say you're kidding me," he moaned when Pier told him of her plans.

"He was deeply hurt and terribly disappointed," Bill Bast wrote. "In his persistent efforts to partake of all emotions to the fullest, when he loved, he allowed himself to love completely, and when he lost the object of his love, he allowed himself to suffer completely." It was a loss Dean never recovered from. Joe Hyams later recalled that a few days before his death, Pier visited Dean at his home. When she left, Jimmy broke out in tears.

Pier was married at St. Timothy's Roman Catholic Church in Westwood on November 24. The marriage was to last only four years. Afterward, Pier would say that James Dean was the great love of her life. It was widely rumored that on her wedding day the actor sat on his motorcycle outside the church, forlornly observing the proceedings. Perhaps that was just a touch of romantic hyperbole; in any event, Dean was not among the six hundred guests who witnessed the ceremony inside the church, the same church where, seventeen years later, Pier's own funeral services would be held after her death, a possible suicide.

# 10

WITH THE LOSS of Pier Angeli, James Dean found himself very much in limbo. *East of Eden* was in the final editing stage, but Warners had not yet decided on another vehicle for him. MGM wanted to borrow Dean for *The Cobweb*, a movie about a deranged artist that Vincente Minnelli was to direct, but Warners balked at the idea of their future matinee idol playing an inmate in a mental institution.

To keep Dean busy the studio lined up several interviews, and the press got its first real look at him.

"I'm a serious-minded and intense little devil," he told Philip K. Scheuer of the *Los Angeles Times*, "terribly gauche and so tense I don't see how people stay in the same room with me. I know I wouldn't tolerate myself."

*East of Eden*, he informed the reporter, was "a study in dualities—that it is necessary to arrive at goodness through a sense of the satanic rather than the puritanic....I considered it a great challenge to reveal honestly the things in [my] part that were of myself as well as the character."

Dean went on to say: "I hate anything that limits progress or growth. I hate institutions that do this; a way of acting...a way of thinking. I hope this doesn't make me sound like a communist. Communism is the most limiting factor of all today."

This was one of only two political statements Dean ever made; in the other he said simply that he "dug Gandhi the most." "He never talked of politics," a roommate, Bill Stevens, later remembered, "and I don't know if he voted or not."

The studio had no control over Dean's TV work, and he was signed to appear with Eddie Albert and Natalie Wood on the *General Electric Theater*. The show, "I'm a Fool, was an adaptation of the Sherwood Anderson story about the folly of a young man in love.

Rehearsals were held in an old theater in downtown Los Angeles, and Dean came late to work the first day. Dressed in a torn sports shirt and pants held together by a safety pin, he made his entrance by climbing through a large window. "I thought he was totally weird—until I began working with him," Natalie Wood later said.

Former president Ronald Reagan, the program's host, remembers: "I was struck by how very much James Dean off camera resembled the James Dean you saw on camera. He worked very hard at his craft, rehearsed with very much the same intensity that he gave the part on camera.... Most of us, after a while in pictures, hold back somewhat in rehearsals and save our punch for the take.... Jimmy did not do this. He seemed to go almost all out any time that he read his lines."

Dean also began to regularly attend an acting class given in Hollywood by Jeff Corey, a stage actor who was then blacklisted by the studios for his political views. Dean participated in class exercises, Corey recalled, trying to achieve more form and control in his own work, and generously gave advice to any young actor who sought it. Later, Corey remembered: "My last conversation with him after class one evening concerned his vexation with a lack of physical specificity in his work. He was certainly aware of his abundance of intuitive qualities but wanted to shape it more. I offered to do some work with him in that area and we agreed to do so as soon as his time would permit. That, alas, along with other things, was not to be."

Dean's social life, too, was far from empty; since losing Pier, he had taken to dating a new girl almost every night, usually starting out the evening with a movie or dinner, and later going to a friend's apartment for coffee. He went out with Lori Nelson, Susan Strasberg, and Terry Moore, to name just a few. But no girl replaced Pier Angeli in his affection; none ever would.

One shapely actress Dean dated was Mamie Van Doren, a fellow midwesterner who was being touted as a rival to Marilyn Monroe. In her autobiography, *Playing the Field*, Mamie recalled that she met Dean one afternoon in a noisy Hollywood bistro, and the actor took her for a spin on his motorcycle through Coldwater Canyon. They pulled off the road and parked in a small clearing, overlooking the city. Dean smoked a cigarette, kissed her, and cupped his hands over her breasts. Then they talked for a while and Jimmy drove her home. She never saw him again; this, no doubt, was a typical encounter for Jimmy.

Around this time, Dean also had a few dates with Terry Moore, another young starlet. Terry was studying with a well-known voice teacher and Jimmy badgered her to convince the teacher to take him on as a pupil. The teacher demurred, claiming she was too busy. Dean persisted, and finally Terry persuaded the teacher to fit him into her schedule. Later, Terry was surprised to learn that Jimmy failed to show up for his first lesson. This also was standard operating behavior.

When the studio finally asked Dean to vacate his dressing room so it could be used for another film, Dean refused. But after he was denied admittance to the gate one night, he was forced to give in. In moving his belongings, it was discovered that Dean kept three thousand dollars tucked away in a desk drawer. He had been meaning to bank the money, he explained casually, but had not gotten around to it; as the story circulated around Hollywood, the amount grew in the telling, adding to the mystique that was starting to spring up around the young actor.

Perhaps Dean's eccentricities were a way of defining his own personality—of leaving behind a trail of stories and anecdotes. "To me, the only success, the only greatness for a man, is in immortality," he is supposed to have told his friend Bill Bast. In Hollywood, no one ever sculptured his own legend better.

By December, Warners had finally edited *Eden* and decided to show a preview at a small theater in Huntington Park. Hollywood was abuzz with the news; for months the town had been hearing of Warners' great new find in James Dean, and at last they could judge for themselves.

Dean invited a number of people to attend the preview, including Connie Ford and her husband, producer Shelly Hull, Bast, and Lew Bracker, a young insurance agent and racing enthusiast he had met during the filming of *Eden*. Two years older than Dean, Bracker was to become one of his closest friends. He was from Arizona originally and had recently been discharged from the army after serving in Japan.

Studio executives had expected the reaction to be good, but even they were unprepared for the reception the movie received. Elia Kazan, who was there that evening, remembered: "The balcony was full of kids who had never seen [Dean] before, [but] the moment he came on screen they began to screech, they began to holler and yell, and the balcony was coming down like a waterfall. Every time he made a move it was like…a landslide." Although the director admitted that he never really liked Dean, he later said, "He made the movie"; and despite his initial misgivings about Dean, John Steinbeck thought his performance was "just right."

Afterward, Dean and his friends crowded together on the sidewalk outside the theater. "Pretty good, wasn't I?" Dean said slyly to one friend. "You're fucking right you were pretty good," the friend replied.

Interest in Dean began to billow. A number of magazines planned stories on him, and Hollywood columnists, who previously had thought of him only as Pier Angeli's boyfriend, requested interviews.

Dean kept Louella Parsons, then the doyenne of the motion

picture press, waiting two hours for a meeting, and when he showed up he was wearing a torn purple sweater and riding breeches out at the knees.

"I can't divert into being a social human being," Dean explained, "when I've been working on a hero, like Cal, who's essentially demonic."

"He's a natural, or a 'primitive,' if you prefer," Louella told her readers in an article entitled, "James Dean—New Face With a Future." "Like the great discoveries before him, he's what makes life in Hollywood exciting." Writer Dorothy Kilgallen prophesied: "He's bound to become a big star—and a big headache."

Although he professed to dislike the press, Dean knew how to manipulate a reporter. According to Joe Hyams, Jimmy would ask the studio press agents to brief him on an interviewer's background so he could tailor his responses to what the reporter wanted to hear. He used this technique to win over Hedda Hopper, then an influential figure in the movie colony who could make or break a career.

Several weeks earlier, Hedda had seen Dean slouching in the Warner's commissary and had dismissed him as another dirty-shirttailed actor from New York. At Clifton Webb's suggestion, however, she saw a preview of *East of Eden* and was captivated by his screen charm.

When Dean showed up at her home for an interview, he appeared as clean-cut and respectful as the boy next door. The middle-aged dowager was favorably impressed. "I want to do *Hamlet* soon," Dean told her. "Only a young man can play him as he was with the naïveté." He added gratuitously, "Laurence Olivier played it safe. Something is lost when older men play him. They anticipate his answers.... This isn't the stumbling, searching boy that he really was."

Hedda urged that some Broadway producer give Dean the opportunity, and thereafter she became his constant champion. "I loved that boy and I always will," she later said. Dean diplomatically referred to her as "my friend at court." Years later, in her autobiography, Hedda described how charming Dean had been at their first meeting. When Rogers Brackett read the story, he called it "a perfect example" of his former protégé's "put-on technique." "She, too, bought the act," he noted dryly.

As the new year approached, Warners still had not decided what Dean's next picture should be. One project under consideration was a film biography of Charles Lindbergh; another was a topical movie on troublesome adolescents to be directed by Nicholas Ray. Juvenile delinquency, then on the verge of becoming a national problem, was very much on the public's mind, and the studio recognized the appeal of a movie on the subject. But Ray had only a rough outline of the film he wanted to do and a title, borrowed from a book Warners owned the rights to: Robert Lindner's clinical study of a teenage criminal, *Rebel Without a Cause*.

Until Warners assigned him to another picture, Dean decided to return to New York to do a TV show and then visit his aunt and uncle in Fairmount. He had been approached by a young photographer named Dennis Stock, who wanted to do a story on him for *Life*, and he invited Stock to come along on the trip. At first, Jimmy tried to hold out for a cover story, but Stock convinced him the *Life* editors would not go for it.

Dean and Stock flew to New York, where Dean was scheduled to appear on the *United States Steel Hour* on January 4. The show, "The Thief," was a routine drama, but the cast was a fine one and included Mary Astor, Paul Lukas, and Diana Lynn. In his TV roles, at least, Jimmy was moving up socially: He played a wealthy young man accused of robbing his family.

Nehemiah Persoff, who was also in the show, remembers Dean was nervous and remote during rehearsals. "Paul Lukas could not stand the way Dean took so much time to do his bit," recalls Persoff. "At one point, Lukas had to face Diana Lynn and say, 'Excuse me, but my son [Dean] is a little peculiar.' At dress rehearsal Dean took a great deal of time, and when

Lukas's turn came he said nothing. The director asked what was wrong. Lukas answered: 'I can't say my boy is peculiar; he is not peculiar. That son of a bitch is crazy."

Shortly after doing the show, Dean and Stock took the train to Indiana.

The trip went well; in Fairmount the prodigal son was welcomed home. The local newspaper sent a reporter to interview him, and everywhere Jimmy went old friends and well-wishers stopped to say hello.

Dean was invited to speak at his old high school, and he gladly accepted the invitation. For an hour and a half he addressed the students as he paced back and forth, reciting Shakespeare, philosophizing, even demonstrating his bull-fighting technique, enjoying himself completely. "He was just a kid showing off for the hometown folks," his mentor, Adeline Nall later said, adding with perhaps more insight than malice, "In a way, that's about all he ever was."

The one-time outcast was now king, and he savored every moment of his triumph.

As ever, the Winslows were glad to have Jimmy home once again. Aunt Ortense cooked his favorite meatloaf dinner, and each night there were extra helpings of mashed potatoes and stacks of fresh cornbread. Among the people he loved and trusted, Dean was open and relaxed. He had recently bought a small tape recorder, and now he secretly recorded family conversations and delighted everyone by playing them back.

For over a week, Stock followed Dean around Fairmount, photographing him against the backdrop of his boyhood haunts, trying to depict the influences and environment that had helped shape the young actor.

Dean had brought his drums along—"to see the farm animals' reactions to a primitive instrument"—and Stock photographed him sitting in a field, surrounded by a herd of cattle as he played the conga drums.

"It was a strange time for Jimmy," Stock later said. "I think that as much as he loved the farm and the earth around it, he realized he had outgrown his past, and Indiana would never really be home for him again."

Stock's many photographs bear out this impression; in them Dean appears almost a stranger, sitting in an empty classroom in his old high school, walking alone across a frozen field, the threat of snow looming in the distance. Even in one picture, taken in the family attic, where he often spent afternoons by himself as a boy, Dean has a blank look on his face, as though the surroundings had become unfamiliar.

On their last afternoon in Fairmount, Dean and Stock paid a visit to Wilber Hunt's general store, a small establishment that doubled as the town's funeral parlor. On a whim, Dean climbed in one of Hunt's coffins and cajoled Stock into taking a picture. "It was the kind of joke Jimmy loved to play," a friend said. "The town thought he was nuts, but to him it was just a prank." To Dean's mild annoyance, *Life* refused to run the shot (Stock's photographic essay "Moody New Star" was published March 7, 1955), but after Dean's death the picture was printed in magazines around the world, a macabre foreshadowing of what had come to pass.

From Fairmount, Dean and Stock returned to New York. Almost from the moment he arrived, Jimmy's spirits seemed to lift. Within a day he was enrolled in a class in modern dance taught by Eartha Kitt and had arranged to take chess lessons. He was, as ever, the young man in a hurry: one book he read was *Learn Chess Fast*.

Already, too, Dean was looking to the future, telling friends that he hoped to someday make a bullfight movie and do a film biography of Woody Guthrie, the dustbowl singer, whose songs he had recently discovered. Ironically, Lon Chapman recalled, Jimmy's favorite Guthrie ballad was "So Long, It's Been Good to Know You."

Eventually, if Hollywood gave him the chance, Dean hoped to one day direct. He bought a Bolex 16mm camera at

Dumont's on 34th Street and began to make his own home movies, using buddies like Marty Landau and Bill Gunn as actors. Naturally, he worked without a script: His muse was the inspiration of the moment.

"Nothing Jimmy ever did was just a sideline," said Roy Schatt, in whose small courtyard Dean made a number of movies. "He put everything he was into everything he did. In his filmmaking, he was constantly searching for the unusual, even the odd camera angle. Sometimes the results were bizarre. But they were always Jimmy." Geraldine Page, who had appeared with Dean in *The Immoralist,* regretted that he died before he could direct any formal productions. Although most of the cast had shunned him, the actress had adopted some of his suggestions in shaping her role. "He would have made a phenomenal director," she later said, "because of [his]...specific kind of ability to excite your imagination without giving you anything that would bind you."

Dean had kept his apartment while in Hollywood, and, as in the past, the small walk-up became a gathering place for his friends. There were long sessions at which Dean played his drums as the New York night wound into dawn through a blue cigarette haze. Conversations ranged from new movies to literature and philosophy. People read stories and plays aloud, once going right through Tennessee Williams's *Twenty-Seven Wagons Full of Cotton* while taking turns sleeping.

During his stay in town, Dean was interviewed by Howard Thompson, then a young *New York Times* reporter. The interview took place in Jane Deacy's apartment. Jimmy arrived late and stretched out on the floor to field questions—a fact that Thompson omitted for the readers of the good Gray Lady. "I got the impression that he liked to act and had made up his mind not to be pushed around by anybody," Thompson remembered. "New York is vital," Dean told the reporter. "I fit to cadence and pace better here. They're a little harder to find, maybe, but out there in Hollywood, behind all that brick and mortar, there are human beings just as sensitive to fertility. The problem for this cat is not to get lost." Later Dean indirectly sent word to the reporter that he "liked the article."

But despite this sudden rush of activity, Dean seemed unable to find real satisfaction in anything he did; the project of the moment might absorb him completely, but he soon grew bored and restless and moved on to something else. His old troubles and anxieties remained, and, if anything, success intensified rather than diminished them.

He was difficult and mistrustful; he quarreled with those around him. "They bum meals from me," he complained. One day in a restaurant he grew sullen. "Where are my friends?" he asked. Four of his closest friends were sitting at the table with him, but before anyone could answer he got up and walked out.

A little thing like a hitch on a telephone he was using could send him into a deep depression, but the mood might lift as completely and mysteriously as it arrived. Once, his friend Tony Ray remembered, his moodiness was cured by going to see Jacques Tati in *The Big Day*. Tati, a Russian-French actor, was known for his comic body gestures and bumbling humor.

Unshaven, hair uncombed, wrapped in his old trenchcoat, Dean was morose as he entered the theater. Within ten minutes he was laughing so wildly that others complained. Dean ignored them; the spell of laughter grew more and more irresistible. But before the film was over he had to leave, making his departure a series of hurdles over the silver ashtrays in the aisle.

While he was in town, Dean also dropped in on sessions at the Actors Studio. Arnold Sundgaard, who had known Dean since *See the Jaguar*, recalled one such occasion: "Jimmy was a name by now," Sundgaard said, "and it was impossible not to glance in his direction. He almost demanded it. He took a seat up front, slouched in his chair with his jacket collar pulled up around his neck. Just like Brando, I thought. He watched the scene being played just in front of him with great concentration—so much so that the collar fell down into its natural place. Moments later, he noticed this and jerked it back to its more sloppy and casual position. And then he resumed the look of concentration." Sundgaard added: "I have seen this a hundred times with other actors in similar situations. They are never 'off.'"

For a time Dean went to an analyst, but when the sessions seemed unable to provide the relief he sought, he stopped going. Frank Corsaro tried to convince him to return, but without success. "He was never in one spot long enough," Corsaro claimed, "and he just seemed to be getting crazier by the minute."

Through a friend, Dean heard that Dizzy Sheridan was in town, and when he got in touch with her, she invited him to a party. Their reunion was a happy one. Jimmy appeared overjoyed to see her and didn't even seem to mind when Dizzy kidded him about the way he was dressed, claiming he looked "so Hollywood" in his black turtleneck sweater.

Later Dizzy recalled: "Wherever I went at that party—if I would go into the kitchen to get food—he would follow me out there and stand and talk. Never anything about Hollywood or what he was doing but what *I* was doing, or how the old gang was. It seemed that he had just been away from home and all of a sudden he returned again and seemed jovial on top—but very unhappy underneath, somehow."

Dizzy also recalled that the newly minted star didn't mingle well with some of her friends. "He wasn't terribly nice," Dizzy said, "and a lot of people left early." He and Dizzy later shared a cab to Grand Central Station, where Dizzy took the train to Larchmont.

"Just before I left," she said, "he squeezed my hand in the cab and asked me if I was happy. I told him that I would be as soon as I could get back to the islands, and he said, 'I know what you mean,' as if more or less he wished he had found a place to go where he could be happy."

Dizzy never saw him again; soon she left for Puerto Rico to take a job with another dance troupe and was living there when

Dean died. The night she learned of his death she had just come out of a movie theater and heard a newsboy shout in the streets that James Dean had been killed in a car accident. The movie that was playing had seen was one that had opened in San Juan a few days earlier, *East of Eden*.

In New York, Dean met another old friend whom he had not seen for some time, but their reunion was less pleasant. Rogers Brackett, who had lost his job at Foote, Cone, & Belding as a result of a cutback at the agency, saw Dean and, over a drink, asked him to loan him some money until things got better. According to Brackett, Dean refused, saying simply, "Sorry, Pops." According to another version, Dean is supposed to have added: "I didn't know it was the whore who had to pay." Dean also told Brackett that he felt he had "outgrown" him and Alec Wilder and no longer wished to be friends. To this, Brackett replied, "You might outgrow me, but I don't think you can ever outgrow Alec Wilder."

Brackett was equally philosophical about the end of their relationship. Later, he explained that he had "other fish to fry." After Dean, and the legend, became famous, rumors about the actor's friendship with Brackett circulated. These were not, of course, the only rumors about Dean's homosexuality. Dennis Stock, one Hollywood friend, claimed that it was a Fairmount cleric who "had first brought Jimmy out." According to another story, a bit player in *Rebel Without a Cause* was Dean's boyfriend. But, even after forty years, only the relationship with Rogers Brackett has been substantiated.

Brackett was always discreet, and after Dean's death, regularly refused press interviews. However, Dean's agent arranged for the studio to pay Brackett a "finder's fee" to allay any bad feeling toward his protégé and safeguard the company's property. After he disappeared from Dean's life, Brackett went on to hold several important advertising positions. Later, he devoted himself to travel, a wealthy, reclusive man who died of throat cancer in 1979. For his part, Alec Wilder never forgave Dean, ostensibly because of his rejection of Brackett. "He was a neurotic, mixed-up kid," the composer claimed. "He bullshitted everybody to death."

By late February 1955, New York was beginning to pale for Dean; the winter had been an unusually harsh one, and he now began to talk of returning to the warmth of California.

The studio, however, was anxious for him to remain in New York to attend the world premiere of *East of Eden* at the Astor Theater on Broadway. The evening was to be a benefit for the Actors Studio. Tickets were priced at fifty dollars a head, and Margaret Truman and Marilyn Monroe were among the many celebrities who had agreed to serve as ushers.

But Dean refused to attend. The studio tried to get him to change his mind, but to no avail. "I can't make this scene," he told his agent, "I can't handle it."

*East of Eden* opened March 9, to much attendant fanfare; over seven hundred guests filled the theater and throngs of spectators lined the police barricades outside to glimpse the event.

But the young star of the evening was nowhere around. Several days earlier Dean had quietly boarded a plane and flown back to California.

## 11

BACK IN HOLLYWOOD, Dean found himself a celebrity almost overnight.

*East of Eden* had opened to great critical acclaim, with reviewers seemingly trying to outdo each other in praising Dean's performance. Writing at length in the New York *Herald Tribune*, William K. Zinnser called Dean's acting "remarkable," claiming: "Everything about Dean suggests the lonely misunderstood nineteen-year-old....When he talks, he stammers and pauses, uncertain of what he is trying to say. When he listens, he is full of restless energy—he stretches, he rolls on the ground, he chins himself on the porch railing, like a small boy impatient of his elder's chatter....He has all the awkwardness of an adolescent who must ask a few tremendous questions and can only blurt them out crudely....You sense the badness in him, but you also like him."

Another reviewer, Kate Cameron of the *Daily News*, was more succinct: "When the last scene faded from the Astor Theater screen last night a new star appeared...James Dean."

As *Eden* opened at other first-run theaters across the country, more praise followed. Herb Lyon of the *Chicago Tribune* credited Dean with turning in "the performance of the year." There was a rave review in *Time*, and *Newsweek* profiled the young actor in its March 7, 1955, issue.

John Steinbeck, who had initially been unhappy with Kazan's decision to use only the latter part of the novel and had absented himself in Europe during the filming, now called *East of Eden* "probably the best motion picture I have ever seen."

By late March, *Eden* had broken into *Variety*'s list of the ten top-grossing films in the country, and soon it was number one. In several cities it set new box-office records.

But despite his newfound fame, James Dean was determined not to become part of the Hollywood scene. In many ways he had never quite gotten over his bitterness at not taking Hollywood by storm after leaving UCLA, and now he was out to get revenge. "They gave me a lot of guff out here last time," he had told Bill Bast some months earlier. "They're not going to do it again. This time I'm going to make sure of it."

"Jimmy didn't go back to Hollywood with a chip on his shoulder," another friend, Vivian Coleman, once said. "It was a boulder."

In public, Dean appeared rude and distant, sometimes deliberately so. He carried around toy automobiles and played with them during interviews while sprawled on the floor.

"You're getting a lot of good publicity these days, all about your wonderful performance in *East of Eden*," a young actress told him admiringly. Dean replied: "Most of it is a bunch of shit."

But whatever his outward pose, Jimmy was not oblivious to his fame. Sometimes he would slip down to the Egyptian Theater on Hollywood Boulevard and stare at his name in lights on the marquee.

At the studio, Dean's behavior became nearly scandalous. He refused to cooperate any further on publicity for *East of Eden*, and began giving out statements saying that acting was not the "be-all end-all" of his existence. Sports car racing was his new passion, he now proclaimed. He bought a four-thousand-dollar Porsche Speedster and let it be known he planned to enter it in local meets.

There was never a dull moment. Lunchtime in the studio commissary could turn into a one-man show, with Dean clowning and banging on the table or sticking a cracker in his eye while eating. "He'd do anything to attract attention," a studio executive said. On one occasion, Dean tore his picture off the wall of the commissary, claiming he didn't want it there; another time he was seen shirtless, eating alone at a table. As if to see how far he could go, he kept a revolver in his dressing room. "We could see then we had a problem on our hands," a Warner executive said simply. The gun was quietly confiscated by the nervous studio.

Dean's conduct aroused much unfavorable attention in the film colony. Hollywood, of course, had always been a split society. On the surface, there was the shimmering image that bewitched the public: the land of beauty, romance, and glamour reflected on the screen. Underneath, there was the dark side, the city of sin and power. Actors and actresses were expected to maintain the image. Public misbehavior was frowned on. One fan magazine bluntly criticized Dean for his "hare-brained refusal to recognize the responsibilities that go hand in hand with being a star." In short, newcomers like James Dean and Marlon Brando mocked the golden myth and enraged the guardians of Tinseltown.

Hollywood columnists characterized Dean as being everything from "uncouth" to "a bit mad." One wag suggested Warners enroll him in a Dale Carnegie charm course, and a magazine editor told a photographer who had done a story on Dean, "I like the pictures, but I can't stand the subject."

Jimmy ignored his detractors. "I came to Hollywood to act, not to charm society," he said, and maintained, "the objective artist has always been misunderstood." He told Bob Thomas of the Associated Press: "I probably should have a press agent, but I don't care what people write about me. I'll talk to [reporters] I like; the others can print whatever they please."

The studio, however, was not averse to cashing in on—even promoting—Dean's offbeat image. One Warner's press release noted Dean's interest in Aztec culture and bullfighting. Written by the talented Ted Ashton, the release had Jimmy saying, "A neurotic person has the necessity to express himself and my neuroticism manifests itself in the dramatic. Why do most act? To express fantasies in which they have involved themselves." To a new generation of teenagers, attuned to the hip and avant-garde, this jargon was music to the ears.

Since moving out of his studio dressing room, Dean had been living in a one-room apartment above a garage on Sunset Strip, about a block and a half from Schwab's drugstore. The small apartment was in such disarray that Dean christened it "a wastepaper basket with walls." Friends said they needed a compass to navigate across it, and one bewildered visitor claimed stepping inside was "like arriving at the scene of a hurricane."

In the evenings, Dean could usually be found at the Hamburger Hamlet, located at 8931 Sunset Boulevard, or at its next-door neighbor, Googie's, a low-price restaurant that was frequented by young actors. Like Dean, Googie's had a person-ality all its own. With its zigzaggy roof and bright decor, it epitomized a style known as Coffeeshop Modern—one of the all-night oases that dotted the Southern California landscape in the 1950s. Dressed in blue jeans and a leather jacket, Dean slumped in a booth in the rear, surrounded by a faithful group of friends. "He was like the maypole, and they were all tied to him," Sidney Skolsky claimed. Since even a few beers made him woozy, Dean drank cup after cup of coffee and chain-smoke (Chesterfields) through the night. "Regardless of how much money he was making, he'd only pay for his own coffee," a crony recalled. "No tax, no tip, and no treating. He was a miser and he hung onto [his] money."

Among the regulars in the group, known as the Night Watch, was an attractive brunette actress named Mila Nurmi. A former exotic dancer and bit player, the lady had a flair for self-promotion that rivaled, and sometimes surpassed, Dean's own. Under the name Vampira she had become well known playing Charles Addams–like characters on a local television show.

One writer called her "the ghoul who gave people right in their own homes their daily creeps." Dean explained their friendship by saying, "I have a fairly adequate knowledge of satanic forces and I was interested to find out if this girl was obsessed with such a force." Vampira put their mutual interests more simply: "We have the same neuroses," she explained.

They had a weird, even macabre, relationship. At their first meeting, Dean took her to his apartment and gave her a Ray Bradbury story to read about a boy who had hanged himself in a garage. When he visited her house, he would climb in through the window. Once he cut up a studio publicity shot of himself, made a montage out of its eyes and ears, and pinned it on her wall as a calling card. (In 1959, Miss Nurmi finally went on to star in a movie, *Plan 9 From Outer Space*. The film garnered a cult following of its own—sometimes respectfully referred to as "the worst movie ever made.")

Stories of Dean's eccentricities began to abound, adding to the growing legend. One evening while dining at the house of actress Terry Moore, Dean put his plate on the floor and began eating "like a cat." This startled Miss Moore, a good Mormon girl, who lived with her mother. On another date, he shocked Terry by undoing his fly.

Another pretty girl recounted to writer Kathryn Tate her own unusual encounter with James Dean: "I was having a soda at Googie's one evening," the young girl said. "Jimmy came in and sat down next to me. I didn't know him personally and he didn't know me. He said, 'Hi,' and started drumming on the counter with the palms of his hands. He didn't say anything else until I finished my soda and got up. 'I'd like to see you again sometime,' he then said. 'Can I call you or come visit you?' Frankly, I was intrigued, and gave him my telephone number and address.

"Twenty minutes later, my doorbell rang. I opened the door and there was Jimmy. He'd brought his bongo drums. He came in, sat down, started playing, and didn't stop for almost three hours. During all that time, we hardly exchanged a word. When he finished, he picked himself up as abruptly as he'd come and left. I never saw him again."

Fortunately, not everything Dean did got into print. One favorite pastime was to get together with a friend from Googie's and go around West Hollywood, trying doors until they found one that was unlocked. If no one was home, they would enter the house, make themselves coffee and fix a sandwich, eat, and then depart, leaving behind a neat stack of dishes in the sink.

Inevitably, Dean's offbeat behavior, as well as some of his mannerisms as an actor, invited comparison with another Kazan protégé, Marlon Brando. "The best way to describe Jimmy Dean quickly," columnist Sidney Skolsky wrote, "is to say he is Marlon Brando seven years ago." One fan magazine even ran a story called "The Boy Who'd Like to Be Brando."

Of all the criticisms hurled against him, being labeled a Brando imitator disturbed Dean the most—perhaps because there was some truth in it. Ever since his early days in New York, Dean had admired Brando and had gotten to know him casually at the Actors Studio, and later at parties they both attended. New York friends recall the zeal with which Dean would rehearse scenes from *A Streetcar Named Desire,* the great Tennessee Williams play that had made Brando a star. In fact, this imitation had carried over to some of Dean's early television work. In reviewing "Death Is My Neighbor," *Variety*'s critic had noted, "Dean's performance was in many ways reminiscent of Marlon Brando in *Streetcar,* but he gave his role the individuality and nuances of its own which it required." Christine White, who was a friend of both Dean and Brando, claimed, "It was a coincidence of nature that they were from the same mold." Nevertheless, Chris remembered that in his New York apartment, amid piles of laundry, Jimmy had a picture of Brando.

The Master, however, was not appreciative. After meeting Dean at a party in New York, he told actress Barbra Baxley,

"You better get him to a doctor, he's very sick." When *East of Eden* was released, Brando publicly attacked his young admirer, accusing him of "wearing my last year's wardrobe and using my last year's talents in the movie."

Such comments stung Dean, although he tried not to show it. "When a new actor comes along, he's always compared to someone else," he told Bob Thomas of the Associated Press. "Brando was compared to Clift, Clift to someone else, Barrymore to Booth, and so forth.... I can only do the best job I can, the realist acting. They can compare me to W. C. Fields if they want to."

But when the comparisons between him and Brando continued, Dean's responses grew icier and more in character. "I was riding a motorcycle long before I heard of Mr. Brando," he pointedly informed one reporter. *Newsweek* reported him as saying: "People were telling me I behaved like Brando before I knew who Brando was. I am neither disturbed by the comparison, nor am I flattered by it. I have my own personal rebellions and don't have to rely on Brando's." On another occasion, Dean announced: "Within myself are expressions just as valid.... And I'll have a few years to develop my own— what shall I say?—style."

The studio was equally eager for Dean to develop his style, and was ready to give him the opportunity. He was awarded a new contract calling for nine pictures over a six-year period, with the guarantee he would receive a minimum of fifteen thousand dollars per picture. The year 1956 was to be open for him to do a Broadway play, and he was free to do any TV work. "I don't have story approval, according to the contract," Dean told Lawrence Boyd of *Motion Picture* magazine. "But emotionally I certainly do. They can always suspend me, for money isn't one of my worries."

Once the new contract was finalized, Dean was assigned to *Rebel Without a Cause*, which had long been rumored as his next vehicle.

Although preliminary work had been underway on the

picture for almost six months, director Nicholas Ray had already had his share of production difficulties. Two early story treatments, including one by Ray himself, had proved unsatisfactory, and he was still without a workable screenplay. Moreover, there were rumblings from the Breen office that any frank treatment of juvenile delinquency might result in denial of a production code seal. At Warners, one or two front-office executives were privately leery about the whole project; some on the lot doubted the film would ever be made. One enterprising technician had even made a sizable bet to that effect.

But Ray was determined to move forward.

A talented, though mercurial, man, then in his early forties, Ray had been educated at the University of Chicago and had had a checkered career before finding a niche as a Hollywood director. He had been at different times a radio script writer, a student of Frank Lloyd Wright's, and a Broadway director before Elia Kazan hired him and took him to Hollywood as his assistant.

Since leaving Kazan, Ray had made a number of notable films of his own, including *The Live by Night, In a Lonely Place,* and *Knock on Any Door,* the last based on Willard Motley's best-selling novel about an adolescent who drifts into crime as a result of poverty. "The protagonist in a Ray film may not have created his torment," writer George Morris once noted, "but he is usually responsible for perpetuating it." To admirers like Morris, Ray was a cinema "poet of anguish and despair."

Not wanting to repeat himself, Ray decided to approach the subject of juvenile delinquency from a different angle, focusing upon middle-class youths whose feelings of isolation and aimlessness placed them at odds with their families and the society around them. It was a theme that was to strike an immediately responsive chord with youthful filmgoers everywhere; bobby socks and penny loafers would quickly give way to the era of blue denim and leather jackets.

To successfully work with Dean, Ray sensed he needed to create "a special kind of climate. He needed reassurance, tolerance, and understanding," the director later wrote. "I leveled with him all the time and made him feel a part of the entire project. He wanted to belong and I made him feel that he did."

Hoping to win Dean's confidence, Ray often invited him to drop by his house on Sunday afternoons to meet his friends and talk. Ray was then living in a small cottage at the Chateau Marmont, a Norman style apartment hotel whose turrets and spires towered above Sunset Strip. The Sunday gatherings included friends like Joe Pasternak, the producer, and screenwriter Joan Harrison, who was Alfred Hitchcock's assistant. "It was exploratory on both sides," Ray said. "Was he going to like my friends, would he find their climate encouraging? Both of us had to know."

One Sunday, after the others had left, Dean found himself face to face across an empty room with Clifford Odets.

"I'm a son of a bitch," Dean said quietly. Odets asked why. "Well," Dean explained, "here I am in this room. With you. It's fantastic. Like meeting Ibsen or Shaw."

Odets afterward remembered this as one of the most charming remarks ever addressed to him.

Another afternoon, Dean met Irving Shulman, who was then working on the screenplay for *Rebel Without a Cause*. Shulman had recently replaced Leon Uris, a contract writer, who had dropped out of the project after contributing some valuable research. He and Ray had visited Juvenile Hall together and had interviewed social workers, psychiatrists— and juvenile offenders—to search for ideas. In interviewing youths, Ray had found the focal point for his movie.

"All told similar stories," he later recounted in *Sight and Sound*, "divorced parents, parents who could not guide or understand, who were indifferent or simply 'criticized,' parents who needed a scapegoat in the family." In 1976, Ray told writer Susan Braudy: "That movie is about a kid who wants to have one day that is not confused."

Reworking the script, Schulman had already made one

valuable contribution, the so-called "chickie run" scene, which was based on a newspaper story the author read. According to the story, a group of teenagers had assembled in stolen cars on a cliff overlooking the ocean. Drivers were to race each other toward the edge, and the first to jump from the car before it went over was a "chickie." On this particular night one of the teenagers failed to jump.

Knowing Shulman was a sports car buff, Ray hoped an immediate rapport would be forthcoming between him and the young actor. The result, however, was disappointing. Dean was dismayed to discover that Shulman's car, an MG, lacked special carburetors for racing and did not have real wire wheels. For his own part, Shulman felt it was "still a little too close to World War II" to appreciate Dean's German-made Porsche. Jimmy typically showed his disapproval by turning away and avoiding further conversation.

Not long after, Shulman dropped from the project to work on a novel; his place was taken by a younger writer named Stewart Stern, who wrote the tender teenage love scenes between Jim and Judy, the two main characters, giving the film an almost lyrical overtone.

In the press there was lively speculation as to who would costar opposite James Dean. Hedda Hopper reported that both Debbie Reynolds and Lori Nelson were under consideration, and another young actress, a comely alumna of Southern Methodist University named Jayne Mansfield, also had tested for the role.

Dean's choice was Christine White, his old friend from the Actors Studio, but ultimately the part went to Natalie Wood, with whom Dean had also worked and liked. A one-time child actress, Natalie was even then only sixteen.

Another former child actor, Sal Mineo, was cast as Plato, the lonely, neurotic youngster whom Dean befriends in the movie. Dean had wanted Jack Simmons, one of the crowd at Googie's, but the studio wouldn't go along. Simmons in fact, was, a close friend who sometimes shared Jimmy's apartment and often followed him around. But when Dean told Simmons of the company's decision, it appeared he was looking out for number one. "I'm under contract with Warners," he said, "and I can't raise too much hell with them."

After meeting Mineo at Ray's apartment, Dean liked him and gave his approval. Mineo revered Dean's memory, but regretted that, because of their age gap, they never became close friends away from the set. Over the years, Sal recalled hearing rumors that Natalie and Dean, or even he and Jimmy, were lovers. Mineo maintained there was no truth to these stories. Still, he always admired Dean. "He was the first rebel," Mineo later said. "He was the first guy to ask, Why? Why?"

In choosing the rest of the cast, Ray also did his best to select actors Dean felt comfortable with.

Nick Adams, a friend from Dean's early days in Hollywood, was signed to play a young gang member, as was Dennis Hopper, an eighteen-year-old actor whom the studio had first spotted playing an epileptic on the television show *Medic* and awarded a contract. He played a gang member named Goon.

Jack Simmons was given a bit part, and Dennis Stock, still another member in good standing of the Dean entourage, became dialogue coach.

Among the "nonclub" members Ray chose were Ann Doran and Jim Backus, who played Dean's parents. Rochelle Hudson was cast as Natalie's mother, and Bill Hopper, Hedda's son, played the father. Marietta Carty, the noted character actress, played a black housekeeper and Mineo's surrogate mother.

By the middle of March, casting was completed and shooting on the movie was scheduled to start at the end of the month.

Before beginning work on the picture, however, Dean planned to enter his first sports car race, an event he had long looked forward to. The meet, to be held in Palm Springs, was sponsored by the California Sports Car Club, an association of amateur and professional drivers.

When the studio got wind of Dean's plans, there was some apprehension in the front office, but director Ray was unalarmed. "I encouraged his racing," he later said. "I felt it was good for Jimmy to do something on his own with clarity and precision."

The weekend of the race, Dean drove to Palm Springs, accompanied by Lili Kardell, a lovely Swedish-born actress whom he had been dating. They planned to stay in a small house in the desert, owned by Dick Clayton, Dean's agent, who was also going to be there with his date. (After Dean's death, Clayton, like Jane Deacy, refused to give interviews about his famous client. Director James Sheldon believed the reason was that neither wanted to answer the inevitable question about Dean's relationship with Rogers Brackett.)

The morning of the race was hot, without so much as a light breeze to stir the desert air. A field of nineteen cars was entered in the competition, a rugged six-lap race over a 2.3-mile circuit set up along the concrete runways of the Palm Springs airport.

Dressed in black racing coveralls and wearing a checkered cap, Dean was in high spirits waiting for the event to begin. "Racing," he would later say, "is the only time I feel whole."

Dean's starting position, drawn by lot, was in the fourth row back, virtually buried behind the rest of the pack. But as the flag fell, Dean jammed his right foot down on the gas pedal and roared away to a perfect Texas start, "stampeding" past a number of other cars by cutting wide around the outside.

"No one expected Dean to go like he did," observed Wilson Springer, a Los Angeles sports car enthusiast. "He went out and left everyone. He was really blasting...going like a bomb."

At the first quarter mile Dean had maneuvered his car into fifth place, and before the first lap ended he had taken the lead. On the long back straightaway Dean was clocked at a hundred miles an hour, the top limit the Porsche could go.

For the remaining five laps Dean easily held the lead, finally taking the checkered flag with almost a full quarter lap separating him and the runner-up.

"He was a lead foot, hard on engines, but he wasn't afraid

of the devil," claims author William Nolan, who was there that day. "Even while charging through the pack, he kept his head sort of slumped down toward his chest and his face was expressionless. You'd think he was out for a Sunday ride. Some drivers frowned, gritted teeth, etc. But not Jimmy. He was totally cool at speed."

In ceremonies following the race, Dean was awarded a handsome silver trophy.

"At first we had thought he was just some Hollywood character out for cheap publicity, but he earned our respect," another driver conceded. "He proved himself one helluva fine driver."

Boosted by his victory, Dean entered another event, a twenty-seven-lap race, open only to professional drivers, and held the next day.

Racing in a much tougher field of competition, Dean finished third behind two top veteran drivers, Ken Miles and Cy Yedor. For his performance, Dean won two more silver trophies: one for his overall third-place finish, and another for taking second in his particular class (cars from 1,100 to 1,500 cc.).

In this race, however, Dean's daredevil élan drew sharp reproach from other drivers. "His skill was a dangerous one," a fellow competitor said. "The kind that comes from a desperate desire to win. He was a menace to himself and other drivers. He would take any kind of chance to be first."

And Ken Miles, an Englishman who was later killed racing at Riverside, summed up Dean's driving this way: "Jimmy wanted speed. He wanted his body to hurdle across the ground, the faster the better. Jimmy was a straightaway driver. His track was the shortest distance between here and there."

But, the race completed and trophies in hand, Dean had other things to think about than the carping of drivers he had handily battled on the track.

That night he had to be back in Hollywood. The next day, Monday, March 28, he had an early date at the studio; shooting on *Rebel Without a Cause* was set to begin.

# 12

OF HIS THREE FILMS, *Rebel Without a Cause*, of course, was the one Dean was most closely identified with. As *Casablanca* was the ultimate Humphrey Bogart movie, so *Rebel* became the quintessential James Dean film—the one in which, the legend maintains, Dean was playing himself: the sensitive delinquent, the original crazy mixed-up kid who, as Pauline Kael put it, "does everything wrong because he cares so much."

The legend is not altogether untrue; so many of Dean's mannerisms—the soft, hesitant drawl, the cigarette dangling from his lips, his perpetual slouch—went into the film that it was difficult to tell where his own personality left off and acting took over. "When you saw *Rebel Without a Cause*," Dennis Stock said, "that was Jimmy you were seeing up there on the screen."

Much of the movie was shot on location in and around the Los Angeles area, using such familiar sights as Santa Monica High School, the Hollywood jail, and the Griffith Park Observatory, where some of the film's most famous scenes were shot. After Dean's death, the planetarium became a mecca for the faithful. In the 1980s, the city erected a bust of Dean, by his friend Ken Kendall, to commemorate the actor's memory. The deserted mansion sequence was shot in the same house where William Holden wooed Gloria Swanson in the movie *Sunset Boulevard*. Now torn down, the old mansion was actually located on Wilshire Boulevard and Crenshaw.

On the set, Dean immersed himself in his role with his usual gusto, sometimes losing himself in the part completely. To key himself up, he would jump up and down, shadowbox, and wave his arms wildly; before doing a difficult scene, Dean would refuse to speak to other actors and demanded total silence, so as not to disturb his concentration. "In the morning when he'd come to work, you could say, 'Hello, Jimmy,' and he'd walk right by you," Dennis Hopper remembers. "But he wasn't really ignoring you.... His approach was to shut the door, and don't bother with anyone.... Just get down to work, because work was the important thing." Jack Holland, a reporter who visited the set was ignored by Dean. His young costar Natalie Wood took the edge off the writer's annoyance by diplomatically explaining: "He lives a part with such verve that it sometimes spills over and seems to injure the feelings of other people without meaning to." Natalie added: "He throws everything into his acting and I have the bruises on my arm to prove it."

More than once Dean held up shooting and delayed production, refusing to work until he was ready. Before doing one scene, in which he is brought into Juvenile Hall on a drunk and disorderly charge, Dean kept the cast and crew waiting an hour while he sat alone in his darkened dressing room, drinking wine and playing his drums to get in the right mood. "What the hell does he think he's doing?" one crew member grumbled. "Even Garbo never got away with that."

When Dean was finally ready, he stormed out, strode onto the set, and did the seven-minute scene in one take.

In shaping his role, Dean drew on his own moods and expressions. There is a scene in which Natalie Wood tenderly tells him of her feelings and asks, "Is this what it is like to love somebody?" When she finishes, Dean drawls softly, "Oh, wow." When Dizzy Sheridan finally saw *Rebel Without a Cause* on television, she recalled Jimmy using that same expression when they were alone.

The movie's plot is a simple one, revolving around a

teenager's first day at a public high school. But underneath that simple theme, the film laid bare the gulf between teenagers and their families. "It's just the age when nothing fits," laments one parent in the film; another asks his child in bewilderment, "Don't I buy you everything...?"

On the surface, postwar America was a placid, well-ordered society; it was a time of expansion and prosperity: the Eisenhower years. But young people coming of age—like those shown in the movie—saw that the honesty and integrity their elders paid lip service to were too often disregarded in reality.

"What can you do when you have to be a man?" Dean asks in the movie. "I want an answer now." On another occasion, he explains to his parents that he took part in a dangerous drag race because, "It was a matter of honor. They called me chicken. I had to go." In another scene, hovering under the dome of the huge planetarium, Sal Mineo says quietly, "What do they know of man alone?"

Teenage audiences totally identified with the movie. The lines Dean—and the others—spoke were in their language, their lingo. "Oh, get lost," Jimmy tells a social worker in one scene, echoing the timeless adolescent desire to rebel against society. If Dean was playing himself, he was playing them, too: kids groping their way in an unloving world, longing for an ideal society where, as Dean's character says at the end of the film, "We are not going to be lonely anymore." In that movie, as in his life, he became as Aljean Meltsir wrote, "the restless emblem of a restless generation." He would be the crown prince of kids who hung out at pizza parlors; a troubadour for youths who dedicated songs to each other on the radio. Their striving for *kicks*—a word a gang member used in the movie— pitted them against their elders who had created what Renata Alder called "the blandest, sanest, most unindividual time in recent memory." If their rumbling was anarchic, it was a cry for freedom, too.

Throughout the filming, Nicholas Ray continued to allow Dean as much freedom as possible in interpreting his role.

"Lack of sympathy, lack of understanding from a director, disoriented him completely," Ray later wrote. "To work with him meant exploring his nature, trying to understand it; without this his powers of expression were frozen."

The director and his young star improvised scenes and reworked the dialogue. Without warning, Dean threw in different lines, keeping the other actors on their toes. Ray understood the need for flexibility in a medium interdependent on writer, actor, and director. "[I]t was never all in the script," he later mused. "If it were, why make the movie?"

When one particular sequence, a scene in which Dean's character quarrels with his father (played by Jim Backus), seemed to be causing trouble, Ray invited Dean over to his house one evening to work on it. When Dean arrived, Ray stationed himself before a television set, switching to a blank screen, so that he could watch Dean unobtrusively as he roamed around, snatched a bottle of milk from the refrigerator, and thought himself slowly in to the situation. After Dean had the scene as he and Ray wanted it, Ray got the set designer to come over to his house so that the living room set for the film could be replaced on the lines of his own; the next day the sequence was shot exactly as Dean and the director had rehearsed it, down to the bottle of milk and the blank television screen that shimmered in the background.

In another scene, a knife fight between Dean and a young gang member, Dean insisted that real knives be used to create the proper atmosphere of tension and danger the situation called for. Over protests from studio officials, Ray backed Dean up; real switchblades were used, and though the actors wore chest protectors under their shirts, Dean received a slight cut on the neck. "Jimmy knew how to use himself with truth and without compromise," Ray later said. It was this, and other scenes in the movie, that led Truman Capote to describe Dean in the *New Yorker* as "the symbol of...hotheaded youth with a switchblade approach to life's little problems."

(Though awarded a production code seal, the film was later

With Pier Angeli

A James Dean
sculpture that
he titled *Self*

Dean's cat, Marcus

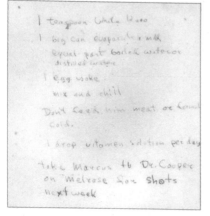

The envelope on which he wrote out Marcus's diet the night before Dean died

A gathering at Googie's. Jack Simmons, who had a small role in *Rebel*, is at the right. (PHOTOPLAY)

With Ursula Andress at Ciro's (DARLENE HAMMOND)

With Sal Mineo in *Rebel*

Revisiting the site of the Winslow farm after wrapping *East of Eden* (DENNIS STOCK, MAGNUM PHOTOS)

Taking dance lessons with Eartha Kitt

Christine White, whom Dean wanted to appear in *Rebel*

With Natalie Wood in *Rebel*

Rogers Brackett in 1974. Behind him is a portrait of himself as a young man. (COLLECTION OF THE AUTHOR)

Elizabeth Sheridan in the seventies

Dean's friend Mila Nurmi, who worked under the name of Vampira

Jett Rink in *Giant* (WARNER BROS.)

On the set of *Giant.* He had a similar noose hanging in his home. (TIME INC.)

An exhausted Dean after finishing *Giant*

In a racing car. "Racing is the only time I feel alive."

Backing the Porsche out of his Sherman Oaks driveway

Dean could be "the boy next door" when he so wished. (WARNER BROS.)

The quintessential Dean in the winter of 1955, just prior to the release of *East of Eden*. (DENNIS STOCK, MAGNUM PHOTOS)

condemned in various quarters because of its violence. Writing in the *New York Times* (October 27, 1955) Bosley Crowther described the movie as "brutal...and excessively graphic," and claimed, "It's a picture to make the hair stand on end." In Memphis, Tennessee, the local censorship board banned the film as being "inimical to the public welfare," and in England, where Dean had numerous fans, it was several years before *Rebel Without a Cause* was allowed to be shown.)

Dean also insisted upon doing his own stunts, even though the production department feared an injury to him might hold up shooting and cost the studio thousands of dollars. In the famous "chickie-run" scene Dean was to leap from a car just before it went over a cliff. The scene was shot at the Burbank studio, and though the car was stationary, Dean refused the use of a mattress to help ease his fall. Limey, the studio prop man, assured Dean that Errol Flynn had used the same mattress in some of his most dauntless screen feats, but the argument fell on deaf ears. "Take it away, Limey," Dean told him. "People will say, 'Jimmy Dean can't even do his own stunts, he needs a mattress.'" The story was duly reported by Sidney Skolsky in his column, "Hollywood is My Beat" (May 27, 1955).

Despite the seriousness with which he approached his role, out of camera range Dean remained unpredictable as ever. "The one thing he could be expected to do was the unexpected," a journalist later noted.

Crossing the studio lot with Stewart Stern after work, Dean was stopped by Warner Brothers executive Steve Trilling and another man. "Here's somebody I want you to meet, Jimmy," Trilling said.

Dean stared at the ground, and acknowledged the introduction by taking some coins from his pocket and tossing them in front of Trilling who was Jack Warner's right-hand man. Then he walked away.

Afterward, he said to Stern, "Stu, I'd like you to do me a favor. If you ever find out why I acted the way I did today, please tell me."

In other moods, however, Dean would graciously talk with fans who visited the set and gladly posed with them for photographs. Once, he delighted a group of visitors by signing autographs to their hearts' content while sitting in an empty trash can.

Jimmy would also entertain others on the set with his excellent imitations, doing Charlie Chaplin, Elia Kazan, or Montgomery Clift with equal ease. One takeoff he did on Mr. Magoo, the radio character made famous by Jim Backus, was so good Nicholas Ray had it written into the script. "He became other people with obvious passion," Ray said. "This was a great part of his magic as an actor."

Along with his pal, Nick Adams, Dean even worked up a comedy routine, and when word got out about it, the two were approached by a Las Vegas talent scout interested in signing them for a nightclub act. Jimmy promised to give it some thought. "It's a lot of money," he told Adams, "and not much work."

Not that Dean lacked other opportunities to pick up a few quick dollars. Early in May, during a break in *Rebel*, he was paid two thousand five hundred dollars for appearing in "The Unlighted Road" on the *Schlitz Playhouse of Stars*. Dean played a young ex-GI who unwittingly becomes mixed up in a hijacking ring. The show, which turned out to be Dean's last television appearance, costarred Pat Hardy. A year later, after Jimmy's death, NBC repeated the program "by popular request." Producer William Self remembers only that Dean "arrived for rehearsal driving a motorcycle. He was extremely casual about everything, but did not give us any trouble." The producer considered him for other shows, but he was not interested.

If Dean could be so relaxed, it was certainly with good reason. He was currently the most sought-after young actor in Hollywood; scripts piled up for him to read, and producers vied to offer him roles. MGM, which had failed to get Dean for *The Cobweb*, now wanted him to play Rocky Graziano in *Somebody Up There Likes Me*, the movie adaptation of the prize fighter's best-selling autobiography. And producer Lew Kerner approached Dean about portraying Studs Lonigan on the screen. Nor were these the only roles believed to be in the offing; even a brief visit the actor made one afternoon to another studio was enough to set off a fresh flurry of rumors. The fact that he was there to see the studio dentist made no difference.

Warners, though, had no intention of loaning Dean out to another studio right now. Although *Rebel Without a Cause* still had several weeks of shooting left, the studio already had firm plans for Dean's next picture. This was to be *Giant*, an all-star vehicle, which George Stevens planned to direct and coproduce.

Based on Edna Ferber's popular saga of a Texas family, the film was to star Elizabeth Taylor, Rock Hudson, and Dean and to feature a fine supporting cast that included Mercedes McCambridge, Jane Withers, Rod Taylor, Carroll Baker, Paul Fix, and Chill Wills. Dean was to play Jett Rink, a bitter and ambitious ranch hand who, through good fortune and a gambling instinct, becomes a multimillionaire. The part was modeled on the career of Glenn McCarthy, the flamboyant Houston wildcatter and builder of the Shamrock Hotel. Known as Diamond Glenn, McCarthy liked to drink and brawl, in that order. Compared to Glenn—a crony once said—"that guy in *Giant* was a sissy." McCarthy built the Shamrock to spite the country clubs that had banned him from membership. The hotel was opened in 1949 with a gala bash that cost a million dollars, an episode that was the inspiration for Dean's drunken banquet scene at the end of the film. For Jimmy, the part was a real plum and a departure from playing what John Dos Passos called "sinister adolescents."

Like Elia Kazan, George Stevens never grew to like Dean. Yet, after Jimmy's death, when Stevens edited the film, he recognized how right he had been to give him the role. As he watched Dean slide across the screen, giggling in a scene, or turning his back to the camera, violating "all the dramatic precepts" of a seasoned actor, he recalled Dean saying when they first met, "Hey, you know something, Mr. Stevens, that part of Jett Rink—that's for me," and imagined him adding in the darkness of the projection room, "I told you it was for me. Man, I just knew."

But if the studio had any hopes that Dean's growing stature as an actor might somehow alter his behavior, they were soon sorely disappointed. At a luncheon given to introduce the cast of *Giant* to the press, it was the same old James Dean who showed up late dressed in blue jeans and his favorite red flannel shirt. While the rest of the cast rose one by one to greet the press, Jimmy sat in his chair and stared at the floor. When a photographer asked him to pose for a shot, the actor clipped on his sunglasses and refused to remove them, explaining he had been up late and had bags under his eyes.

Dean also continued to avoid the usual Hollywood social scene, preferring instead the company of cronies like Lew Bracker, stunt driver Bill Hickman, and Bill Stevens, a sports car driver who was then sharing Dean's apartment.

Stevens had a girlfriend who was a secretary, and he and Dean often double-dated, with Dean going out with one of her friends. Stevens, who afterward became an actor, always looked with amusement on stories that linked Dean romantically with Natalie Wood. "Natalie was just a little girl then," Stevens said. "Jimmy and I used to walk her home from school."

Dean's favorite date was Lili Kardell, whose lively outlook and cheerful antiestablishment attitude closely resembled his own. "With Jimmy nothing was ever planned; everything had to be spontaneous," remembers Lili. "I would get on the back of his motorcycle and he would go like hell." Knowing the way to her man's heart, Lili, who is now an interior decorator in New York, once sent Dean a new oil filter for his Porsche as a gift.

Always on the lookout for a new home away from home, Dean began to take his meals at the Villa Capri, a small Italian restaurant located on McCadden Place, half a block from Hollywood Boulevard. The maître d', Nicolas Romanos, was something of a character in his own right. An engaging White Russian emigré, Romanos claimed to have once been a dancer with Diaghilev's Ballet Rousse and to have hobnobbed with various legendary figures as a young man in Paris.

The first time Dean came to the restaurant and asked what was good on the menu, Romanos told him, "How should I know? I hate Italian food. Go down the street to Don the Beachcomber's if you want a good meal." After that, Romanos quickly became both Dean's friend and confidant, and the Villa Capri his new hangout.

Dean invariably entered the restaurant by coming in through the kitchen, first stopping to sample the antipasto the chef kept in the refrigerator. If the restaurant was crowded, Jimmy simply sat at a table reserved for someone else. Finally, Romanos resolved matters by fixing up a small storeroom off the kitchen where the actor could eat. Sitting there on an empty orange crate, he could enjoy his veal parmigiana apart from the other diners.

Dean's mannerisms, however, were no longer much of a novelty. Fewer eyebrows were raised when he sauntered into his favorite places unshaven and wearing a string, instead of a belt, to hold up his pants. At the Villa Capri Dean might sit alone for an hour, carefully building a house out of breadsticks, but no one paid much attention. What had once been ways of expressing his identity now seemed only a calculated pose to get attention.

There were some, of course, who felt this was what Dean had been up to all along. "He was always conscious of his image," a director claimed, "and he worked very hard to maintain it."

"Dean could behave intelligently when it suited him," explains Walter Ross, who was then a publicity man at the studio. "If there was something important he wanted to talk to you about, he expressed himself clearly, but after he told you what he wanted, all you would get from him was mumbles. It made you wonder." Ross, who eventually left Warners to go out on his own, later wrote a novel, *The Immortal,* in which the main character, a brash young actor, reminded many of Dean. (The book also fictionalized Dean's involvement with the smart, gay crowd that had revolved around Lemuel Ayers and Rogers Brackett.)

By now even some of Dean's closest friends were beginning to be put off by his antics. "It was the same game he had been playing for two years," declared Bill Bast. "I was embarrassed by his lack of inventiveness, and it bored me."

Although Bast's affection for his friend still remained, other friendships proved not quite so durable. There was a falling-out with Vampira that delighted the film press. "I don't date cartoons," Dean told one reporter. Over the years, Vampira paid him back, chipping away at the legend. "He was attracted to—whomever," she once said, hinting at Dean's bisexuality.

Dean's friendship with Leonard Rosenman, a young composer who had scored *East of Eden,* also ended abruptly. Rosenman, who was then engaged in scoring *Rebel,* had once been as close to Dean as anyone; at one point the two had talked about Dean directing a one-act opera, *Cipolla the Great,* that Rosenman had written, but this, too, died with the friendship. Even after Dean's death, some of the bitterness lingered. "Jimmy was always saying how he loathed Hollywood," Rosenman told writer Martin Mayer, "but really he loved it. You know how it is, in the land of the blind the one-eyed man is king. In Hollywood, Jimmy could believe he was an *intellectual.*"

Shooting on *Rebel Without a Cause* was completed the last week in May, and Dean immediately reported to start work on *Giant.* Stevens and the other principals in the cast planned to leave on the twenty-seventh of the month for Charlottesville, Virginia, where the movie was to be shot on location for two weeks. Since Dean was not needed for any scenes there, Stevens arranged for him to remain behind, getting outfitted for his wardrobe and working with dialogue coach Bob Hinkle to perfect a Texas accent. Dean was then to catch up with the others in Marfa, Texas, where principal location work was scheduled to begin early in June.

Once again, however, the subject of Dean's racing came up. Several weeks earlier, midway through *Rebel Without a Cause*, he had shaken front-office executives by entering his car in a Sunday meet near Bakersfield. Driving on a rain-slicked track, Dean won two trophies in an afternoon that was marred by a crash in which a thirty-two-year-old driver, Jack Drummond, lost his life. When a reporter asked Dean how Warners felt about his racing he replied: "They sort of shoot around it, but they've never said, 'Don't do it.' Everybody likes a winner, and so far I've been winning."

But now George Stevens put his foot down. A five-million-dollar production was at stake and Stevens had no intention of jeopardizing it for Dean's love of speed: During *Giant* Dean was forbidden to race or to take his Porsche with him to Texas as he had hoped. He had told the director he wanted to use the car to hunt rabbits, but in Marfa, Dean would have to find other means for getting around on the range.

Although he had given his word to Stevens, Dean conveniently managed to stretch his side of the agreement. Memorial Day Weekend (May 28–29) there was a race being run in Santa Barbara, and he decided to compete in it, though work in *Giant* was officially under way. He once said of racing: "If I thought I was risking my life, I wouldn't participate. I love life too much. There are too many things I have to do."

Accompanied by Bill Stevens, his friend and mechanic, Dean drove to Santa Barbara the day before the race and checked into the Del Mar motel.

The next morning Jimmy was at the track early. "I saw him at the technical inspection," said driver Dave Watson. "He was…off to the side by himself. He was very interested in the other cars. I could tell he didn't miss a trick."

But luck was not to be with Dean that weekend. He drew a poor starting position, finding himself eighteenth behind the leader at the pole.

Pushing hard from the outset, Dean maneuvered his car through the crowded field, moving ahead until another Porsche suddenly cut in front, nearly brushing his bumper. Dean swerved to avoid a crash and sideswiped two of the packed hay bales, skidded for several feet, and came to a halt. According to William Nolan, who witnessed the event, only Dean's quick reflexes and thinking averted a catastrophe.

Immediately Dean resumed his former pace, and by the fifth lap he had moved into fourth place, gaining rapidly on the leader. But Dean was pressing too hard, and his engine blew under the strain. With a single lap remaining, he coasted to a halt at the side of the track, his dicing at an end. The race was won by Dale Johnson, a driver Dean had beaten at Palm Springs.

Back in Hollywood, Dean had no time for bitter reflection. With only a week left before he was due in Marfa, he settled down to the serious business of tackling his role. He read up on Texas history and studied a tome on cattle raising. He put his tape recorder to good use as well, spending hours going over his dialogue.

The part of Jett Rink, Dean freely admitted, was the hardest challenge he had yet faced. Still, on the eve of his departure his enthusiasm remained high. "George Stevens is the greatest director of them all—even greater than Kazan," he asserted. "Stevens was born for the movies. You know, when it wants to, Hollywood can accomplish tremendous things. And this movie might be one of them."

This was indeed heady praise, and a rare song for James Dean to sing, but down in Marfa there would be a more familiar tune.

# 13

FIFTY-NINE MILES from the Mexican border, and three and a half hours by car from El Paso, the nearest city of any size, Marfa, Texas, was a typical sleepy Southwest town. The population was approximately twenty-nine hundred; the mayor, Henry A. Coffield, had recently been reelected to office without opposition, and the surrounding area, Presidio County, was in the grips of a severe drought.

Some 280 strong, including technicians and actors, the company of *Giant* poured into town, bringing with them over a million dollars' worth of equipment to mount the production. To capture the flavor of life among the Texas rich, the studio imported a fleet of expensive automobiles, including a grand 1924 Rolls-Royce touring car. A three-story Victorian mansion, which had been built at the studio in Burbank, was shipped to Marfa in sixty sections and reassembled on a ranch seventeen miles outside of town. Costing $200,000, the building was used only for exteriors and remained behind after the filming; the ranch's proprietor, Ward Evans, later converted it into a hay barn.

Ironically, Marfa is situated in an area of West Texas that produces no oil—the terrain is rugged mountain country; so the company erected its own wells, machines that gushed over twenty-two hundred gallons of ersatz oil a minute. To simulate a dust storm for one scene, a gigantic wind machine was also constructed, but here Marfans were on more familiar ground and remained unimpressed. One old-timer who had seen many a real duster called the Hollywood facsimile "a pretty puny attempt," complaining it hardly stirred up "more than four acres of soil."

But generally relations were good between the movie people and their hosts. Edna Ferber's novel, which some had thought a roman à clef about the King Ranch, had not been popular among Texans, who considered it an unflattering portrait of their state. According to a Dallas newspaper columnist, one Texan had threatened, "If they make and show that damn picture in Texas, we'll shoot the screen full of holes." The film company was prepared to go to great lengths to ensure local harmony. The set was thrown wide open to visitors, who came from all over the state to see the filming, in some cases timing their summer vacations so they could make the trip.

To further cement good relations, a former rodeo queen from the University of Texas was signed for a cameo, and in one barbecue scene, it was said that among the sixty-five extras ten were authentic Texas millionaires. One, Fayette Yates, happily announced that he had finally fulfilled a lifelong ambition to be an "actor." The pride of Texans was a serious matter and would not be treated lightly by their Hollywood brethren.

In Marfa, this strategy worked especially well. Altogether, almost two hundred Marfans went on the company payroll, including the town's lone bootblack, whom director Stevens personally invited to be in the movie "along with Rock and Liz." He played a train porter.

The town's weekly newspaper, the *Big Bend Sentinel*, which had once denounced Edna Ferber's novel as "superficial and derogatory to Texans," now was won over to the side of the angels: "The filming of *Giant* has brought invaluable publicity to Marfa," a writer neatly explained, "in addition to putting many thousands of dollars in circulation."

Although Stevens retained the good will of Marfans

throughout the filming, achieving peace within his own company proved somewhat of a different matter.

The movie was on location slightly more than two weeks when the first reports of dissension between Stevens and Dean filtered back to Hollywood.

Then fifty-one years old, George Stevens had a solid reputation as a Hollywood director, having made such movies as *A Place in the Sun,* based on Theodore Dreiser's *An American Tragedy,* and *Shane.* A one-time cameraman who had first broken into movies shooting Laurel and Hardy comedies, Stevens's directorial method was both expensive and time-consuming—as well as enormously successful. Known as the "round the clock" system, Stevens would shoot a scene from every conceivable angle and spend up to a year editing the footage, selecting the best frames for his final print. (On *Giant* over 600,000 feet of film were shot, of which 25,000 were used.)

Sets and location were his staple, Cinemascope, his wizardry. "The concentric classicism of the Stevens frame," critic Andrew Sarris noted, "once looked like an official style for national epics." In *Giant,* he sought to capture the struggle between oilmen and cattlemen, old money and new, a theme big as the Texas range. At one point in the movie, Dean says: "I guess Christmas is as good a day as any to talk business." In another scene, he tells a cattleman bluntly, "I'm going to have more money than you ever thought you could have."

On the set Stevens was regarded as a taskmaster who had firm ideas of how a scene should be done and very little patience for actors' vagaries. Dean, on the other hand, worked best in an informal atmosphere, one in which he was free to improvise.

"When an actor plays a scene exactly the way a director orders, it isn't acting. It's following instructions," Dean maintained. "Anyone with the physical qualifications can do that. [An actor] must be allowed the space, the freedom, to express himself in the role. Without that space an actor is no more than an unthinking robot with a chestful of push buttons."

In *Rebel Without a Cause*, Nick Ray had allowed him such freedom and achieved fine results. But Stevens had no intention of permitting his twenty-four-year-old star any such liberties. In her autobiography, *Baby Doll*, Carroll Baker recalled: "There are many directors...who would have been phony with Jimmy in order to get a performance, appeasing him on the set and then complaining bitterly about him behind his back." But not ex-Army officer Stevens. "He told Jimmy what he thought of his conduct to his face and never changed that story when relating it to others."

In recounting his experiences in working with Dean to a *Saturday Review* reporter, Stevens had this to say: "[Dean] had the ability to take a scene and break it down; sometimes he broke it down into so many bits and pieces that I couldn't see the scene for the trees, so to speak. I must admit that sometimes I underestimated him, and sometimes he overestimated the effects he thought he was getting....All in all it was a hell of a headache to work with him....It's tough on you, he'd seem to imply, but I've just got to do it this way. From the director's point of view that isn't the most delightful sort of fellow to work with...."

Frustrated by his lack of rapport with Stevens, Dean quickly lost interest in the production. He avoided the rushes, which were shown each evening at a local theater the company took over, and absented himself from social gatherings attended by the rest of the cast. At one barbecue he did go to, Dean filled his plate with fried chicken and repaired to a cowshed, only emerging after most of the others had left.

Rock Hudson, who was assigned the same living quarters as Dean, later complained that he never got "a single pleasant word" from him. Working with Jimmy did not give him much pleasure. Doing a scene with another actor, Hudson said, usually involved "giving and taking." Dean was "just a taker." According to one account, Hudson hadn't forgotten that Dean was once a bit player in a movie he had starred in, and resented the attention Dean was receiving in the press. But whatever the reasons, the dislike was clearly mutual. "He was nasty, mean," Hudson told reporter Maurice Zolotow. "I don't know what was eating him. If I said hello or good morning, he snarled at me."

Later Zolotow was disturbed—if not infuriated—by the Dean legend. He considered Dean to be "a second-rate actor" and blamed the studio's publicity department for building him up as a "romantic rebel" to promote *Giant,* which was released a year after the actor's death. Zolotow labeled Dean "a rotten hero"— "rude," "sexually twisted," and "abusive" to those around him. In 1956 he wrote prophetically in the *Los Angeles Times* "The persons whom youth idealizes exemplify certain traits which unconsciously shape the lives of children as they grow up. To some extent, what our country will become tomorrow is determined by whom our children admire today." It may be that the hero of the fifties sowed the seeds of rebellion that were to flower in the free spirit of the sixties and seventies.

With several exceptions, Dean's relations with others in the company were not much better than those he had with Hudson. Chill Wills, who also had been bunking with Hudson and Dean, soon moved out after an argument over Jimmy's playing a guitar. A man of few words, Wills had taken the guitar and broken it. In the movie he played a hard-drinking cowpoke. In old age, he later campaigned for George Wallace for President. He and Dean had little in common. One night Dean showed up wearing a headlamp strapped to his head and toting a .22 rifle he used to shoot jackrabbits. "These Actors Studio kids are a weird bunch," Wills complained to a reporter, Elston Brooks of the *Fort Worth Star Telegram.*

Fortunately, Dean had a number of allies on the set. Dennis Hopper, his friend from *Rebel Without a Cause,* had a supporting role in *Giant* and was also on location in Marfa. Six years Dean's junior, Hopper had grown up on a small Kansas farm, and their similar backgrounds drew him and Dean together despite the age difference. "It wasn't a buddy-buddy hang-out thing," Hopper later explained. "But he knew I was really interested in acting and film, and it became sort of like student and teacher between me and Jimmy."

On *Rebel* Dean had offered Hopper an occasional acting tip, introducing him to fundamental Method techniques. "If you're smoking a cigarette, smoke the cigarette and don't *act* [it]," Dean had told him. "You have to do something and not show it."

But in Marfa he began watching Hopper's takes, sometimes without Hopper's knowing it, and afterward they'd go over the scene.

"He was the most creative person I ever knew," Hopper later said, "and he was twenty years ahead of his time."

Dean's self-assurance before the cameras also impressed his young protégé. "Jimmy would come on the set and literally give everybody the finger and make them his enemy," Hopper told an interviewer for *Gallery* magazine. "Then he wouldn't have to hear from the grips about how James Cagney would have played that scene or listen to all the advice a young actor would have to stand...from the crew." This admiration, however, may not have been mutual. Dean's Hollywood roommate, Bill Stevens, remembered: "He was very fond of Dennis Hopper when Dennis first came to Warner Brothers. That didn't last too long, as Dennis began to change. But I think Dennis greatly admired Jim."

So great was Dean's influence that after his death Hopper seemed determined to carry on in his friend's footsteps. He moved to New York to enroll in the Actors Studio and remained there two years. When he returned to Hollywood to make a western, he quickly earned a reputation as being difficult to direct. As a result, Hopper worked very little over the next decade, landing only an occasional part in low-budget productions (*Night Tide, The Trip*), until he teamed up with Peter Fonda to direct and act in *Easy Rider*, a motorcycle opera about life in the sixties. The movie grossed millions and made Hopper a star in his own right, though in numerous interviews he always acknowledged his debt to Dean, faithfully maintaining his position as Dean's self-appointed heir for over a quarter century.

But Dean's influence had more immediate results as well. Inspired by his friend, Hopper sometimes resisted Stevens's suggestions, wanting to play a scene his own way. This did not please the director, who believed in "the teamwork of moviemaking." "You've been watching that Dean again," Stevens would tell Hopper sternly. "You guys are screwing me up."

Elizabeth Taylor, who was having her own share of differences with Stevens, likewise found a friend in Dean. Originally, Stevens had wanted Grace Kelly for the movie, but when she proved unavailable, he turned to Liz instead. He had directed her in *A Place in the Sun* and had gotten a good performance from her as a spoiled heiress, but her role in *Giant* was far more demanding. She played a woman who ages thirty years in the course of the film, going from an eighteen-year-old belle to a grandmother of two. At the time, Liz was only twenty-two, which made the latter transitions in age that much harder to portray. (Carroll Baker, who played her daughter in the movie, was twenty-four.)

Like Dean, Taylor found herself at odds with the director. "I found out on *Giant*," she later explained, "that [Stevens] tends to like having a patsy or two on a film. James Dean was one and I was another, but I'll say this for George—he usually picks people who can answer back."

One early skirmish took place over a costume Stevens had selected for her. Taylor claimed the heavy stockings and large hat the director had chosen made her look mannish. Stevens charged that all she cared about was how she looked and that her only concern was in "being glamorous." "There was a huge battle," Liz remembers. "I think I got rid of the hat. Nobody won; nobody lost; we did the scene. It was like that during the whole film."

Liz's friendship with Dean did not go unnoticed by the Hollywood press. In the movie, Dean played a rough outsider who loves the cattle baron's beautiful wife, played by Taylor, from a distance, and reporters in Marfa, seeing Taylor and Dean having dinner at a local county club, or strolling through the streets of town, naturally hinted at a possible romance. These rumors were helped by the fact that Miss Taylor's marriage to English actor Michael Wilding, her second husband, was known to be on shaky grounds. Others, however, believed there was no substance to the rumors. According to John B. Allan, one Taylor biographer, her friendship with James Dean was similar to the one she enjoyed with Montgomery Clift, with whom she had made *A Place in the Sun* and who had remained her dearest friend. "If the relationship with Clift was like two cousins who'd met after both had grown up," Allan wrote, "the relationship with Dean was more like two in-laws, neither of whom can stand the rest of either family."

Most of Dean's free time, however, was spent in the company of Bob Hinkle—a former rodeo rider whom Stevens made the cast's dialogue coach—and with other cowboys and stuntmen. Carroll Baker wondered if "that is how rumors of [Dean's] homosexuality got started," but concluded (probably correctly) that Jimmy's motive was only to learn from them. Before the start of the picture, Hinkle had worked with the actor on his accent, and in Texas the friendship deepened. "People told me he was moody and hard to get along with, that he clammed up and wouldn't talk," Hinkle said. "That was a lot of nonsense. He could talk your arm off."

Hinkle, who was from Brownfield, Texas, taught Dean to ride herd and rope cattle, and even how to spot what area a Texan hailed from by the crease in his hat. Sure enough, Dean soon announced that he and Hinkle were planning to enter a major rodeo in San Francisco in the fall. This, no doubt, was another of Dean's momentary inspirations that delighted studio publicists by providing good copy: like Dean's plans to study music in Haiti or even return to school for law.

Nevertheless, Jimmy dutifully practiced the rope tricks Hinkle showed him. "I taught him how to build a loop with the rope," Hinkle said. "There's a lot more to it than just making a big loop. You have to work it so that you can throw it off your hand just right. Before we came back to Hollywood, Jimmy was an expert." Dean neatly employed his newly acquired skill in the movie; in a scene with Rock Hudson he nonchalantly performed a rope trick while delivering his lines. It stole the scene. Even Stevens was not impervious to Dean's insight and dedication to his role. "He used himself as a kind of clay," the director said. "It was his finest art."

At sundown after a hard day on the set, Dean and Hinkle would climb into the company car and drive off into the prairie to hunt jackrabbits. Often he and Hinkle stayed out all night returning to the location after dawn. Dean would later show up at breakfast and announce to the others: "We killed 34 rabbits last night; that makes a total of 104 to date." Then, he'd turn and leave.

Maybe it was the Texas sun; maybe it was the boredom of the high desert or the endless takes that Stevens exacted, but Jimmy's behavior seemed to slip from the offbeat to the bizarre. He boasted that he cut off the ears of rabbits he had killed and planned to send them to Jack Warner. Once, it was reported that he took a break during rehearsal and urinated in front of the startled crew. Another time (back in Hollywood), he reached under a table during a scene and grabbed Carroll Baker's crotch while she struggled through her performance. "There were many things about this boy that many people wouldn't have overlooked," Henry Ginsberg, the film's coproducer, said later. "I overlooked them because he had talent."

This sentiment was echoed by actress Mercedes McCambridge: "I can't tell you how he needed to be patted," Miss McCambridge said afterward. "He was the runt of the litter of thoroughbreds. You could feel the loneliness beating out of him, and it hit you like a wave.

"You can forgive a lot of things for talent, and Jimmy was bursting with it."

June had been hot in Marfa, but July was even hotter. By early morning the temperature was already in the eighties and in the afternoon the mercury climbed well past ninety.

After four weeks of being on location, the cast had grown weary and restless. Despite the hospitality of Marfans, supper dances at the local Lions Club had no further allure, and the visitors yearned for the excitement of Hollywood.

After a final week of shooting in the broiling Texas sun, the last location footage was in the can, and by July 8 the company was free to depart. Two months of filming remained to be done back at the studio in Burbank, but Mr. Stevens's movie was right on schedule.

# 14

IN HOLLYWOOD, Dean quickly got back into the old groove, dropping by the Villa Capri for dinner his first night in town and calling friends to let them know he was back. One girl he called upon his arrival home was a shapely Swiss-born actress he had met the day before leaving for Texas. Her name was Ursula Andress, and she also was a friend of Dick Clayton's. In true Hollywood storybook fashion, their first date was chronicled in detail in *Movie Stars Parade*.

Later famous as a James Bond heroine, Ursula was then a nineteen-year-old starlet who had only recently arrived in this country and was under contract to Paramount. The studio had discovered her in Europe, where she had appeared in several Italian-made quickies like *The Many Loves of Casanova*. Until she learned to speak English better, Paramount was keeping her under wraps, hoping to eventually groom her as another Marlene Dietrich.

On their first date, Dean had come by for Ursula an hour late. "He come in room like wild animal and smell of everything I don't like," she complained in her German accent. "He stalked all through my house...then sat down on the sofa and sat staring at me saying nothing." When they started talking, they immediately got in an argument over music. "It was then I first felt like an American," Ursula said. "In Europe a woman does not argue with a man."

They joined friends for dinner and afterward went to a

club on Sunset Strip to hear jazz. The band allowed Dean to sit in with them, and he spent most of the evening playing the drums. "I don't like to be alone, so I went home," Ursula said. About an hour later Dean drove up on his motorcycle, and after apologizing, convinced her to go for hot chocolate. They came back to her house, and sitting on the curb, talked until 5:00 A.M.

That same day Dean left for Texas, but as soon as he returned, he and the starlet picked up where they had left off.

"We would fight, then make up, then fight again," Ursula recalled. She also remembered that "he always drove like a maniac." They argued about anything and everything, everywhere they went. Jimmy complained that Ursula's German shepherd was eating him out of house and home. "It'd be cheaper to have a family," he told her. At the Villa Capri he objected when Ursula ordered steak. "It's costing me five dollars every time I take you out. Why can't you eat spaghetti for sixty-five cents?"

"We fight like cats and dogs. No—on second thought, like two monsters," Dean admitted. "But then we make up and it's fun. Ursula doesn't take any baloney from me and I don't take any from her. I guess it's because we're both so egotistical." They both were eccentric, too. In quieter moments they could be seen sitting in the Villa Capri, barefoot, surrounded by curious diners.

Throughout that summer, their romance was on again, off again. "I tried to love him, but it didn't work," Ursula later commented. She claimed that she was not ready for marriage and that he "was too unstable." One story has it that she was finally stolen from Dean by John Derek, the handsome actor who sponsored her career, as he was later to do with another beauty, Bo Derek.

Ursula Andress, however, wasn't the only female with whom Dean was having a personality conflict; for some time he and his landlady had been having a dispute over his odd hours and late-night bongo sessions, and Dean finally decided to move. Some months before, he had taken an option on Lana Turner's former home atop Laurel Canyon, but changed his mind when a columnist printed an item about it and tourists began flocking to the site. Now he looked elsewhere.

Nicolas Romanos, the maître d' at the Villa Capri, had recently put his home in the San Fernando Valley up for rent and moved to the beach, so that his wife, Grace, who was in poor health, could be near the ocean. Romanos had been having trouble renting his house, but as soon as Dean saw it he decided to take it.

The home, which was destroyed in a fire several years later, was located at 14611 Sutton Street in Sherman Oaks, a quiet residential neighborhood.

Built to resemble a hunting lodge, it had a large living room with a seven-foot stone fireplace, a small dining area, and a kitchen. There was no bedroom, but a small balcony that jutted out over the living room had a cot on which to sleep. When Jimmy climbed into bed, he had to crawl through a trap door.

The place had come furnished, but somehow everything in it seemed to fit its new tenant's personality to a tee: In the living room there was a white bearskin rug, an old-fashioned wheel lamp hanging from the high ceiling, and a huge bronze eagle Dean immediately dubbed "Irving." Dean was delighted with the home and took great pleasure in showing it off to friends, always demonstrating how he climbed into bed by means of a wooden ladder.

Otherwise, however, things were not going quite so well.

On *Giant,* Stevens and Dean had not managed to resolve their differences, and to make things worse the director was faced with new problems. Elizabeth Taylor had suddenly been hospitalized for a blood clot in her leg, the result, she claimed, of having worn jodhpurs that were too tight. The blood clot proved not to be serious, and Stevens was able to shoot around Taylor until she was released from the hospital.

But no sooner was she back at work than she suffered an attack of sciatica (severe backache) and had to be briefly hospitalized again. This time, however, Stevens did not learn of his star's hospitalization until he read about it in the papers, and when he did, he was convinced it was psychosomatic. Stevens's diagnosis was backed up by several doctors, but even so, when Liz returned to the studio she had a nurse and wheelchair ready in case her pains returned. (Later, when she learned of Dean's death she broke down and was hospitalized a third time.)

Meanwhile, the situation between Stevens and Dean was deteriorating daily. The early flareups in Texas now seemed mild compared to the range war that was about to erupt.

Starting the last week in July, Dean had a series of early-morning calls that required him to be at the studio at 6:30 A.M. and made up by 9:00 A.M. Twelve- or thirteen-hour days were the usual routine: The old Master didn't kid around. For several days Dean managed to show up on time and ready for work, but by the end of each day his scene still had not been shot. Upset, the actor complained to a friend that he had "sat for three days…like a bump on a log watching that big, lumpy Rock Hudson make love to Liz."

Convinced that Stevens was trying to punish him by deliberately postponing his scene, Dean decided to boycott the studio and take a day off for each one he had sat idle. "I am not going to take it anymore," he told a pal.

The following morning, true to his word, Jimmy failed to show up for a scheduled scene. Frantically, the studio put in a call to his home and finally reached him at 4 P.M. According to a studio memo, Dean explained casually that when he got up that morning he was "too tired to work." His absence cost the studio thousands of dollars in wasted time.

Word of Dean's rebellion spread throughout Hollywood. Columnist Sheila Graham printed a detailed account of the incident, upbraiding Dean as "a young so-called star who after a year in pictures wants to teach, instead of learn." Even the studio's reaching Dean on the phone, she informed her readers, had been "no mean feat in itself, for Dean guards his...number with the same secrecy the government puts on its nuclear developments. And even when his right number is reached, he may let it ring for hours and never answer it. Maybe he just likes to hear bells ring."

Lest anyone miss her point, she added: "I'm getting a bit weary of the offbeat characters who work their heads off to get to Hollywood and then turn around and pretend that this isn't what they want at all. Jimmy Dean is a prize example."

At Warners, Dean was given a firm dressing-down by Stevens, but apparently he was still not ready to capitulate; several days later he was back on the carpet again, this time for being late on the set.

Dean had been scheduled to do a scene with Mercedes McCambridge. Miss McCambridge had slipped in her tub that morning and had cut herself badly, requiring several stitches, but she still managed to make it to the studio on time. Then she and the rest of the cast had to wait for Dean. When he finally showed up, the director berated him for five full minutes in front of the entire company. Stevens lit into Dean for his "inconsideration" and told the young actor he had never seen anyone "go Hollywood" in such a short time. As Stevens stormed off the set, he vowed Dean would "never appear in another film I do." Once again, Dean was roundly knocked in the press.

Hedda Hopper, Dean's staunchest supporter, rallied to his aid. "Jimmy Dean was late for work one day and you'd have thought he'd committed a crime," she wrote in her column, assuring Stevens, "He's worth waiting for, and I'm predicting he'll steal the picture to prove it."

But the director's tirade worked; knowing when he was licked, Dean gave in, coming as close to apologizing as he ever would. "The trouble with me is I'm just dog-tired," he told Dorothy Manners. "Everybody hates me and thinks I'm a heel. They say I've gone Hollywood, but honest, I'm just the same as when I didn't have a dime. I went right into *Giant* immediately after a long, hard schedule on *Rebel*. Maybe I'd just better go away for a while."

The rebellion quelled, and, Dean back in the fold, the director was quick to forgive. He denied the young actor was on any blacklist for future movies. "A lot of stories going around have been built on minor things," Stevens told the *Los Angeles Mirror-News* in a story that ran on August 5, 1955. "The boy's so preoccupied, he's the kind that can be late even if he's right there on the set...But his work is wonderful," the director added. "Everything went fine when we shot all night at the Statler and Jimmy even showed up for makeup call fifteen minutes early."

## 15

HAVING LOST THE BATTLE as well as the war at Warners, Dean readily found a sanctuary in the quiet of his new house. Friends often dropped by for late-night talks or to drink wine and listen to records on the new hi-fi system Dean had recently installed. Two large speakers hung down from the beamed ceiling; neighbors claimed the music could be heard five blocks away.

The refrigerator was well stocked with hams Uncle Marcus sent from the farm, and Dean was building a trophy room in the cellar with the help of Nick Adams. Intense and ambitious, Adams was very much like Dean, and later went on to a successful career of his own, playing off-beat parts. He had hitchhiked to Hollywood at eighteen, determined to make it as an actor. "Some men bet on horses and dogs," he liked to say. "I gambled on myself." After Dean's death, he was always ready to give an interview about his lost friend; some were quite imaginative. In one such interview, he quoted Jimmy as saying, "There are six needs in life: love, security, self-esteem, recognition, new experience, and last but not least, the need for creative expression." Adams also died young, in 1968, of a drug overdose, at the age of thirty.

Mike Connolly, a magazine reporter who dropped by to interview Dean early in August, was surprised to find him so friendly and relaxed. Jimmy was dressed in a white Mexican shirt and jeans. He put on a pot of coffee, and gave the customary tour of the premises, proudly pointing out the apple and lemon trees that bloomed in the backyard. When the reporter noticed a hangman's noose strung from the ceiling beam, and a sign—WE ALSO REMOVE BODIES—tacked next to it, Dean chalked them up to "my macabre sense of humor."

The windows and doors were thrown wide open; Bach's *Toccata in F Major* blared on the hi-fi. A white bearskin rug was thrown across the floor; the bear's ferocious jaw stretched open. Jimmy was once photographed playing his drums next to the rug; a careful look at the photo shows his foot sticking in the bear's rear. It is a picture (taken by Stanford Roth) that still shows up in novelty shops. To the end—and beyond—he was non-Hollywood all the way.

Dean and Connolly had a long talk about music over coffee. As they talked, Jimmy kept changing records, going from Bartok to African chants to an old Jimmie Rogers record he had picked up in a secondhand shop. Dean explained that Rogers was a great "hillbilly" singer who died in his early thirties. He added: "But folk singers still worship at his shrine."

"I collect everything from twelfth- and thirteenth-century music," he boasted proudly, "to the extreme moderns—you know, Schoenberg, Berg, Stravinsky. I also like Sinatra's *Song for Young Lovers* album."

Among Dean's closest friends there was now a growing feeling that somehow Jimmy had changed. One humid night, sitting in his kitchen with Lew Bracker, Dean turned and said quietly, "You know, Lew, I think we ought to get married."

"To each other?" Bracker joked.

"No. Seriously," Dean replied. "I mean it would be so right to come home to somebody who understands me, who cares."

Dean was a many-sided figure: manipulative, talented, even touched by genius. Yet, the side Bracker saw was that of a friend. Bracker's cousin was then married to a composer whom Dean was close to. When the composer began a relationship with another woman, an actress who had appeared in *East of Eden,* Dean voiced his disapproval out of loyalty to the wife.

Bracker, who later became a Beverly Hills investment banker, was then living with his parents in Studio City, and to them Dean practically became one of the family that summer. "He'd come to the house," Bracker remembers, "with a bucket of peaches he'd picked from his tree for my mother. Or he'd bring a couple of pounds of hamburger and insist on cooking dinner for us....At first, if we had other people in, he would sit in a corner of the yard by himself. But toward the end, he was getting better....He'd join the other people and joke with them."

Dean's attitude toward Hollywood had softened, too. There was not much surprise when Dean began showing up at the better-known night spots, or was seen around town escorting actresses like Leslie Caron, whom he took to see the movie *Summertime.*

When singer Ella Logan took over Ciro's to host a party for Sammy Davis Jr., Dean dropped by and mingled easily with the other guests, one of whom was Humphrey Bogart. Like Googie's Ciro's has since become part of Hollywood folklore— a glamorous nightclub where stars and stargazers spent enchanted evenings. Later, Bogart, the old pro, said: "Dean died at just the right time. He left behind a legend. If he had lived he'd never have been able to live up to his publicity."

Yet, underneath it all, the rebellious spirit had not died. In one of the last interviews he did, with a writer named Jan Jamison, James Dean summed up his feelings, striking a note that might have served as an epitaph. "If a choice is in order— I'd rather have people hiss than yawn," Dean claimed. "Nothing can be more deadly than boredom, and this applies if one is either the cause of it or its victim." He added: "My purpose in life does not include a hankering to charm society....Of course, I am well aware that there are those who think a net should be dropped over me. But any public figure sets himself up as a target and that is the chance he takes. Most of us have more than one choice and I chose to be what I am, rather than remain a farm boy back in Indiana....Despite endless odds and issues along the way, I've never regretted it."

Writing that summer to his old friend, Reverend James DeWeerd, Dean reached ever deeper inside himself. "I don't really know who I am, but it doesn't matter," he admitted. "There really isn't an opportunity for greatness in this world. We are impaled on a crock of conditioning. A fish that is in water has no choice what he is. Genius would have it that he swim in sand....We are fish and we drown."

But that summer Jimmy allowed himself little time for such melancholy thoughts. He was involved in a host of new activities, learning tennis at the venerable L.A. Tennis Club, studying German ("so Ursula and I can fight better"), laying plans for the future.

In August, Dean told friends that he soon hoped to form his own production company, working with Warners as an independent producer. He talked about doing a short of a Bartok ballet, *The Miraculous Mandarin*, and wanted to film *The Little Prince*.

He had other ideas as well: a life story of Tazio Nuvolari, the Italian racing ace who had been nicknamed the Devil's Son, and who had been buried in his racing helmet, a steering wheel beside him. Another potential project was a film on Billy the Kid. Dean said he would make the latter movie only "if I can do it honestly," portraying the outlaw as a cold-blooded killer rather than a romantic hero.

The old spirit and drive had returned—to have tomorrow today, to live two years for every one.

On the set of *Giant* Dean became friendly with Sanford Roth, who had joined the company as still photographer after their return from Marfa. Roth, who died in 1962, was a former merchandising executive who had given up a successful business career to become a professional photographer. He and his

wife Beulah had lived in Europe for a number of years, and he
had done a book on Paris with Aldous Huxley.

When Dean learned Roth knew and collected the works of
artists like Miró and Picasso, he asked: "When can I come and
see you?" That same night he went to the Roths' West Hollywood home for dinner and stayed till five in the morning.

After that Dean was often in their company. He took them
to the Villa Capri for dinner, and some evenings they would all
go over to Will Wright's for ice cream. Whenever Mrs. Roth
knew Dean was coming over, she liked to make what soon
became his favorite snack: Jewish salami toasted on Italian
pizza.

The Roths stimulated Dean's yen to travel and introduced
him to the writings of avant-garde writers they admired: Jean
Genet, Curzio Malaparte, and Gerald Heard, the English
scientist, who was then living in Hollywood.

Along with Roth, Dean visited a Buddhist temple in
downtown Los Angeles, observing a class of kendo, the Japanese art of self-defense. Naturally, Jimmy became enthusiastic
about learning the sport and wanted to take lessons.

When Roth mentioned that he knew of an old hotel in
Venice, a local beach community, where Sarah Bernhardt had
once stayed, Dean insisted they drive out to see it at once. It was
late at night, but they managed to rouse the desk clerk to show
them the room. Dean was thrilled to sit on the bed in which the
great Bernhardt had supposedly slept.

"He knew the world was round," Roth said, "but he never
stopped trying to prove it to himself." Like Dennis Stock and
Roy Schatt, Sanford Roth became one of James Dean's court
photographers. He shot numerous photos of Jimmy—twirling
a lariat, caressing his drums, even sitting with a cat on his
shoulder: cool, studied poses that later helped market the
Dean legend.

Since Beulah Roth's brother, Leonard Spiegelgass, was a
close friend of Rogers Brackett, the Roths presumably knew of

Dean's relationship with the director. In fact, in later year Spiegelgass told his sister he felt that Dean had behave "treacherously" toward his mentor. But Brackett's name wa never mentioned in the books or articles the Roths did o Dean.

Rogers himself never became a Dean "fan." With regard Dean's film work, he was simply noncommittal. As for th legend, it perplexed him. He found most articles on Dea filled with "inaccuracies and half truths." Once he sent a pal clipping on Dean with a note, "Another item from th morgue." When Brackett learned that in the 1970s Dean autograph had sold for more than one of Lincoln's, he note wryly, "I wish I had saved J.D.'s love/hate letter and poetry an drawings—I'd take a world cruise on the proceeds." The lette he referred to was one that Dean had written after they sai their good-bye. A few years after Dean's death, Rogers threw out, along with other Dean artifacts.

It was Dean, the person, that he knew and remembered. I the 1970s he saw a TV movie about Dean written by Bill Bas The sanitized memoir greatly amused him. "What a fantasy, he told a writer friend. "It should have been called *Mothe Cabrini—Girl Saint*." Chris White, who was in the cast, re marked that actors kept coming up to her saying, "Are you th real Chris White?" She felt it was "all kind of unreal, being par of a myth." Naturally, Rogers Brackett was unmentioned in th production.

After Dean's death, magazine articles appeared with title like "How Should He Be Remembered?" and "You Can Mak Jimmy Dean Live Forever." Mike Connolly noted in the *Holly wood Reporter:* "A lot of characters who knew [Dean] onl casually—or not at all—are writing articles or even book about him. After all, who can check?"

Early in September 1955, Sandy Roth introduced Dean t Pegot Waring, a West Coast sculptress, and Jimmy asked her t take him on as a student. "Acting is just interpretation," he told her. "I want to create myself."

After his third lesson, he wanted her to explain the technique sculptors used to carve Mount Rushmore. "He asked a hundred questions," she later told reporter Aljean Meltsir. "He always wanted to know why? why? why?"

Dean worked on a bust of Elizabeth Taylor and one of Edna Ferber, who was in town checking on the progress of the movie. The frail, elderly novelist was captivated by Dean, calling him "utterly winning one moment, obnoxious the next."

"Your profile resembles that of John Barrymore," she told him, adding sadly and prophetically, "but then, your automobile racing will probably soon take care of that."

# 16

By September the subject of racing was very much on Dean's mind. So far he had kept his promise to Stevens, but Dean's impatience was growing. He had missed the Hansen Dam race in June and the Torrey Pines contest in July. Over Labor Day he had attended a race in Santa Barbara, watching Lew Bracker drive. As a favor to the car club, Dean had gone on Tom Harmon's KNX sports show to promote the event. Driver Jim Matthews recalls: "Dean's answers to questions were, 'Yes' or 'No.' He seemed incapable of ad-libbing. I heard the program and nearly cringed in sympathy for Tom. Pulling words out of Dean was like pulling teeth. Tom was POed at Dean and furious with me for setting up the interview."

As sometimes happens, Tom Harmon's perception—and recollection—were different from Matthews's. In 1974, the former Michigan football hero recalled: "I had been told that Dean would be difficult but I found him just the opposite. He chattered like a buzz saw and was very engaging in his conversation....As I recall, James Dean seemed excited about the silent battle and danger that all race drivers know. I think Dean accepted that fact of a driver's life and readily enjoyed flirting with danger."

Dean had loaned Bracker his racing helmet for good luck, but his friend did not have one of his better days, finishing twenty-fifth in a field of thirty-nine. He was sixteenth in class F.

Back from Santa Barbara, Dean spoke constantly of racing and the events he planned to enter once *Giant* was completed, as it soon would be. There was a rugged road race, the Carrena Americana Mexico, that Dean had set his sights on. The two-thousand-mile race was run down the Pan American Highway, and simply to finish was an achievement. But the race was run irregularly; no definite date had been set for the next event, and in the meantime there were other club meets the actor planned to enter. He told columnist Harrison Carroll in mid-September: "I want to enter at Salinas (on October 1), Willow Springs, Palm Springs, all the other places." Jimmy added that he was going back East later in the fall for some television work, but "maybe I can catch a race back there." When Carroll asked if Warners approved, the rebel finally drew the line. "When a man goes home at night," he replied, "the studio can't tell him not to do what he wants to do."

Since his return from Marfa in July, Dean had been shopping for another car, one with more horsepower and a finer racing edge. He had put a small down payment on a Lotus Mark IX, a British racer, planning to put an Offenhauser engine in it.

But now, through Lew Bracker, he heard of another car, a Porsche 550 Spyder that Bracker had spotted in the window of Competition Motors on North Vine Street.

The car was a beauty. It cost six thousand nine hundred dollars and was capable of 150 miles per hour. Its body was made of thin aluminum and had no windshield or bumpers; only seventy-five of these cars had been manufactured by the Porsche factory in Stuttgart. "This is strictly a racing car," Dean said. "It goes like a bomb. It'll be very hard to catch."

Jimmy traded in his old Porsche Speedster, paying the difference. Before completing the deal, however, Dean insisted that Rolf Weutherich, a young mechanic at the shop, promise to accompany him to his next race and check the car before he competed. Weutherich, a thin former Luftwaffe pilot who had recently come to this country from Germany, readily agreed.

The mechanic had seen the actor race and admired his driving. "He was one of the best drivers in California," Weutherich said. "He had that essential feel for fast cars and dangerous roads. When he drove, he drove with his whole being. He had steel in his hands."

The deal was completed the same morning Dean visited the shop. It was Monday, September 21, 1955.

The next two weeks were busy and crowded with activity. *Rebel Without a Cause* was sneak-previewed in Westwood, near UCLA, and Jimmy went with several friends. "He was sitting there just behind me," Sal Mineo recalled, "and half a dozen times when he was really terrific I turned around and looked at him. He was giving that grin of his and almost blushing, looking at the floor."

In 1976, shortly before he was tragically murdered—a victim of random violence—Mineo was to say: "I still am emotionally unable to watch reruns of *Rebel*. I still talk of Jimmy to my closest friends, still find myself thinking of him at odd moments, still run into complete strangers who ask me to tell them something about Dean."

Jimmy's own verdict was that the movie was good but could have been better, and that he was dissatisfied by a number of his own scenes. Afterward, he told Dennis Stock he was a bit put off by Nicholas Ray's Hitchcock-like appearance in the movie. In the film's final frame the director is seen walking toward the planetarium with his back to the camera.

But, for the moment, Dean kept the comment to himself, and after the preview, Ray, Dean, Natalie Wood, Sal Mineo, and Nick Adams—the whole gang—went to Googie's for a midnight celebration.

Largely as a favor to Lew Bracker, Dean had recently taken out a $100,000 life insurance policy with Bracker's company, Pacific Indemnity, and one afternoon Bracker brought the policy by the studio. Dean signed the policy, telling Bracker he wanted the bulk of the money to go to his aunt and uncle, and the rest to be distributed among his relatives in Indiana.

Bracker explained that he should make a will, specifying each amount. Dean agreed, but never followed through, and on his death his entire estate went by law to his father.

Jane Deacy, Dean's agent, had come to town for several days on business, and Dean was happy to entertain her. He met her at the airport and filled her Chateau Marmont suite with flowers and candy.

Miss Deacy got right to work negotiating a new contract for her client with Warners. Dean's base salary for *Giant* was fifteen thousand dollars—though an overtime clause raised the figure to nearly thirty thousand dollars—but in the future he would receive one hundred thousand dollars per film.

Miss Deacy had also lined up two television specials back in New York. One was a dramatization of *The Corn Is Green* with Judith Anderson, to be done on NBC in late October. Dean was to play Morgan Evans, the young Oxford-bound coal miner's son. The other show was A. E. Hotchner's adaptation of the Hemingway short story *The Battler*, in which Dean would play Ad Francis, the battered prizefighter.

In addition, MGM had gotten Warners' approval to borrow Dean for *Somebody Up There Likes Me*, which was scheduled to go before the cameras in January. Dean had read Graziano's book and liked it. "What a guy," Dean said. "One day when he was in the Army, he got tired of it and just got up—walked out—went over the hill. The army never forgave him....You've got to admire that kind of nerve."

Dean met Dore Schary, the head of MGM who approved him for the part. Decades later Schary still recalled the outfit Dean wore that day he dropped by for the interview: jeans, Indian moccasins, and sunglasses—his James Dean wardrobe. As Jimmy strolled around, casually examining the well-appointed office or picking up objects on the desk, Schary found him "a strange combination of immaturity and aggressiveness." Dean made sure MGM would match his hundred-thousand-dollar salary. The studio boss also mentioned that Pier Angeli had been chosen to play Graziano's wife and that Sal Mineo, another Dean friend, who had a cameo in *Giant*, was going to be in the cast. Mineo later remembered that "Dean was looking forward to doing the film since he knew Pier was in it."

Dean's future appeared secure. The starving artist had never been his métier. Now, he was willing to capitalize on his fame; the carrions of Hollywood were there to oblige. He was asked to endorse a clothing line and talked about obtaining a Porsche dealership to be called Jimmy Dean Motors. A Beverly Hills business management firm was called in to help handle investments.

On Friday, September 23, Dean was having dinner at the Villa Capri. Sir Alec Guinness, who had only arrived in Hollywood that day, was there, and Dean asked Sir Alec to join him. "You are my favorite actor. I'd like to meet you," Dean said. Guinness found Dean "very agreeable," and the two talked casually about actors and acting. Dean insisted on showing him his new Porsche, which was parked outside. "When he told me the speed he wanted to go in it," Guinness remembered, "I begged him never to get into it. Something made me say: 'If you do, you will be dead in a week.'"

This was not the first premonitory warning, nor was it the last. Several days later Dean offered coproducer Henry Ginsberg a ride to the studio, and when Ginsberg got there, he told the production department: "If you have any loose ends, you better tie them up quick. The way this kid's handling that car I don't think he's going to be around much longer."

The next day Dean completed his work on *Giant*. This was the famous banquet scene in which Jett Rink collapses and passes out in front of a packed ballroom. Later, Lee Strasberg was to say that this was "an enormously difficult scene" that Dean had played "superbly." Although *Giant* was his favorite of Dean's three pictures, the tough teacher still felt that his pupil never "achieved the fulfillment that he was capable of as an actor."

To make him look older and more dissipated, Dean's hair

had been shaved back and dyed gray. Jimmy kept missing his lines and the scene had to be reshot several times until Stevens ordered it printed. Stevens, though was still not satisfied with the print, and after Dean's death, Nick Adams was quietly brought in to dub additional dialogue.

Afterward, Stevens was to say of the young actor and his growing legend: "He'd hardly broken water, flashing in the air like a trout. A few more films and the fans wouldn't have been so bereft. This first bright phase would have become an ordinary light and wouldn't have produced this kind of thing." He also said: "Jimmy had no will to die. He was very much planning for the future.... He was a boy with a wonderful sense of the theater. All this encourages young people, particularly young actors, to behave eccentrically. They saw it paid off for Jimmy."

But, for Dean, his commitment on *Giant* was officially over. He was now free to race.

Looking forward to the big event on Saturday, Jimmy invited several friends to go along with him, but for a while it didn't look as though he could get anyone to go. Nick Adams was leaving for New York to be with Natalie Wood, and Lew Bracker had tickets for the USC-Texas game. "Okay," Dean told him. "It's your funeral."

Bill Stevens told Dean he couldn't leave Friday morning as Dean planned, but would drive to Salinas that night and be there in time for the race the next day. Stevens was packing his bags for the trip when he learned of Dean's death. "If I was with him it wouldn't have happened," Stevens remembered sadly. "I never let him drive that way."

Finally, Dean convinced Bill Hickman to accompany him, and photographer Sandy Roth, who was doing a story on Dean for *Collier's*, agreed to go too.

On Wednesday, September 28, Dean relaxed much of the day, then went to the movies that evening with Ursula Andress and Lew Bracker to see *I Am a Camera*. The film and play of the same name were based on a novella by the English writer

Christopher Isherwood, who then lived in Santa Monica. Jimmy pretended to know and admire him. A few weeks earlier, Dean had even promised to introduce his pal Bill Bast to him. Later it turned out that Isherwood had never met the actor. To the end, it seems, Jimmy never outgrew his fondness for exaggeration.

Thursday, he drifted around town, appearing at Warners around noon in his car. He talked with Stevens a few minutes, then drove off, telling the director, "So long, I think I'll let the Spyder out."

For several days, Dean had been toying with the idea of driving the car to Salinas himself instead of towing it on a trailer. Driving around Hollywood he had only managed to put a couple of hundred miles on the odometer, and Weutherich, his mechanic, felt he needed to drive the car at least five hundred miles to properly learn to handle it. Thursday, Dean definitely decided to drive the car himself.

Late in the afternoon, Dean picked up Bill Hickman to drive up the coast to Santa Barbara to put more mileage on the car.

"In those final days, racing was what he cared about most," remembers Hickman, who later did the stunt driving in *The French Connection* and who died of cancer in the 1980s. "I had been teaching him things like how to put a car in a four-wheel drift, but he had plenty of skill of his own. If he had lived he might have become a champion driver. We had a running joke, I'd call him Little Bastard and he'd call me Big Bastard. I never stop thinking of those memories."

The car handled well on the road to Santa Barbara, but when fog rolled in from the ocean, Dean was forced to turn back. Driving back to town, a highway patrol car followed them for speeding, but the Porsche managed to outrun it.

That evening, Dean stopped by the apartment of Jeanette Miller, a young actress who was another of Dick Clayton's clients and whom Dean sometimes dated when he and Ursula were on the outs. Several weeks before, Elizabeth Taylor had given Dean a Siamese kitten, which he named Marcus. Because he was going out of town, Jeanette had agreed to take the kitten and Dean brought it over. Jeanette had been looking at an old movie on television, *The Boy With Green Hair*, but Jimmy was too restless to watch the picture. Jeanette later said of their relationship: "We talked a lot. We laughed a lot." But that night Jimmy appeared "tense" and "irritable." They talked for a while, and before leaving the apartment around 9:30, he wrote a formula for feeding Marcus on the back of an old envelope.

"Be careful at the races," she said.

"Sure," he drawled softly. Then he kissed her on the forehead, scratched the kitten, and left.

When Dean got back to his house, he phoned his father and asked if he wanted to attend the race. Winton Dean declined the invitation, but promised to drop by Competition Motors the next day, along with Dean's uncle, Charles Nolan, who was visiting from Indiana.

Too keyed up to sleep, Dean drove his Porsche up to Coldwater Canyon and raced along the narrow road. Below the lights stretched the reach of the valley toward the shadows of the distant mountains. Then, he finally returned home.

Early Friday morning Dean was awakened by Nicolas Romanos, who often dropped by to fix breakfast and straighten up the house. The actor was still groggy from lack of sleep.

"He didn't say hello," Romanos remembered. "He never would. He kept his drums at the bottom of the stairs and he would sit down and beat them. He would never talk until his coffee was ready."

Dean left the house at 7:45, dressed in blue jeans and a T-shirt. Romanos stayed behind to clean up and put the breakfast dishes away.

It was a warm morning. Dean drove his Ford station wagon to Hollywood, the Porsche mounted on a trailer behind. On the side of the Spyder he had painted his racing number, 130, and across the rear he had written the nickname "The Little Bastard."

Dean was at Competition Motors by 8 A.M. According to Aljean Meltsir, who wrote a detailed account of that day, Weutherich went immediately to work, checking the Porsche over. Dean paced the floor, then came over and asked the mechanic if he needed help. "No thanks," Weutherich joked. "You'll only complicate things."

Dean went into the office and thumbed through the newspaper, but within a few minutes he was back, looking impatiently over Weutherich's shoulder.

When the mechanic had finished checking the car, he attached a safety belt across the driver's seat. Since Dean was going to be alone during the race, he didn't fix one for the passenger's seat. Dean sat in the car and tried the belt.

Around ten o'clock, Hickman and Roth showed up at the shop. They were going to take the station wagon on the trip. The mechanic would ride in the Porsche with Dean.

A few minutes later, Dean's father and uncle walked in. Jimmy offered to take his uncle for a ride, and they drove around the block a couple of times.

At noon, Weutherich went home to change clothes, and Dean and the others went to the Hollywood Ranch Market, half a block away, for coffee and donuts.

When they got back to the shop, Dean told his father he had an extra ticket if he wanted to see the race, but Winton was unable to make the trip; several hours later, when Dean's body was taken from the wreckage, he still had the ticket in his pocket.

At one-thirty they were at last ready to leave. Jimmy clipped on his sunglasses and tossed his red jacket in the backseat; the safety belt remained unfastened. Winton and his brother drove off. Roth photographed Dean and Weutherich as they sat in the car, hands clasped above their heads in a victory salute.

Afterward, George Stevens would say Dean "worked hard to get publicity and always had a photographer with him." The trip to Salinas was no exception.

Traffic was heavy as the two cars drove out to Ventura Boulevard toward Highway 99 (now Interstate 5), which cuts through the mountains between Los Angeles and Bakersfield.

The sun was high in the afternoon sky. Sometimes the Porsche led, sometimes the station wagon moved out in front as they headed toward the mountains.

Dean smoked cigarette after cigarette, which Rolf lit for him, all the while pumping the mechanic with questions about how the car was operating.

Rolf finally closed his eyes against the sun's glare and leaned his head back, almost lulled to sleep by the soft purr of the motor.

Dean was happy behind the wheel. The wind rushed by as they wound through the mountain range that brushed against the sky. "Life is wonderful," Dean is supposed to have murmured.

A few minutes before 3 P.M., they stopped near the top of Ridge Route at a roadside place for something to eat. Dean had a glass of milk and Rolf ordered a dish of ice cream. The mechanic warned Jimmy not to go too fast during the race the next day. "Don't try to win," he told him. "It's a big jump from a Speedster to a Spyder. Try for second or third. Drive for the experience."

"All right," Dean replied. "You give me the pit signals."

A few minutes later, Roth and Hickman came in and ordered sandwiches. When they finished eating, they all left the restaurant.

Back on the highway, the Porsche was quickly in the lead. The car wound down the mountain and raced along the flat, dusty plains. A highway patrol officer, O. V. Hunter, flagged down the car for speeding. Dean was given a ticket for doing sixty-five in a fifty-five-mile-per-hour zone. Jimmy explained to the officer that the Porsche wouldn't perform well if driven under sixty miles per hour. The cop advised him to go slower anyway. Roth and Hickman, who had pulled up alongside in the station wagon, were also given a summons.

Before they drove off, Dean and the others decided their next stop would be for dinner in Paso Robles, 130 miles away.

Dean headed toward Bakersfield. They drove through the town, with its broad, palm-lined boulevard, and moved west, past the black oil pumps and balls of tumbleweed that dotted the highway. The land was bare, burnt brown by the September sun. Only a farmhouse or two stood in the empty fields.

As Dean approached Blackwell's Corners, a gas station—general store perched along the highway, he spotted a Mercedes 300-SL and pulled off the road to examine it. The car belonged to Lance Reventlow, Barbara Hutton's son, who was also on his way to the meet, along with race driver Bruce Kessler. Jimmy and the two drivers talked for a while; they too had been ticketed for speeding earlier. It had been a busy afternoon for the highway patrol.

Before the two left, Dean told Kessler that he had hit one hundred miles per hour on the open stretch of road between Bakersfield and the Corners.

Roth and Hickman arrived in the station wagon. Roth bought a bag of apples for the road. "How do you like the Spyder now?" Dean asked, his face flushed from the sun. "I want to keep this car for a long time—a real long time."

Dean bought a Coke and shared his cigarette with Hickman; then he got back into the Porsche. His safety belt remained unfastened.

"See you in Paso Robles," he yelled to Roth. Later, Hickman told writer Paul Hendrickson: "The way he died was grim, fatalistic—proof of everything people were saying about him. The mythmakers had what they wanted."

On Highway 466 (now 46), Dean continued west. The setting sun loomed over the mountains in the distance, shining in his eyes. The narrow road curved through the hills, then dipped to the Cholame Valley and the farmland below. The wheat and barley had been harvested in the surrounding countryside, and the brown, flat fields stretched toward the horizon.

Dean pressed forward, invited by the open road. The Porsche hugged the ground, its silver body, the traditional German racing color, blending into the land as the car raced through the valley.

At a narrow intersection in the road, about thirty miles from Paso Robles where Highway 466 met Highway 41, a Ford, driven by a young Cal Poly student named Donald Turnupseed, prepared to turn left.

Dean saw the car too late, crying out as it hurled into them. The impact tore the left front fender off the Ford. The Spyder was thrown in the air and cartwheeled along the ground, coming to rest near a telephone pole. The crash threw Weutherich nineteen feet from the car. His jaw was broken and his hip fractured in several places, but he recovered. (In later years, he became a rally driver for Porsche and was killed in an automobile accident in Germany, in 1981.)

Turnupseed suffered minor injuries; an inquest was held but he was absolved from blame. He later said that the accident happened "in a snap of a finger."

Dean's body lay twisted in the car. His neck was broken and his chest crushed where the steering wheel had smashed into him.

He was pronounced dead on arrival at a nearby hospital.

On October 8 funeral services were held at the Friends Church in Fairmount, Indiana, where Dean had worshiped as a boy.

Some three thousand people, more than the entire population of the town, turned out to pay their last respects. The church was filled with family and friends, and hundreds of others gathered outside.

There was very little evidence of Hollywood glitter. Henry Ginsberg was there representing the cast of *Giant* and Elizabeth Taylor had sent an arrangement of orchids. The accompanying card said simply, "With love always, Elizabeth."

Ginsberg knew that Dean had been difficult on the set; later, he would say simply that the young actor "had his peculiarities." But in Fairmount, he spoke only good of the deceased star. The producer told the townsfolk that Dean "was not only well liked, but highly respected by his fellow workers in the movie industry. He was adjusting himself well to his sudden rise to stardom."

A handful of Dean's personal friends—Lew Bracker, Nick Adams, and Dennis Stock—came to say good-bye.

The Quaker service was a simple one. The Reverend James DeWeerd, Dean's boyhood friend, read a brief eulogy. "We cannot measure a life in years, moments, days, or minutes," he said. "Although Jimmy's life was a short one, he accomplished more than most persons do if they live to be seventy or eighty."

The organist played "Going Home" from Dvorak's *New World Symphony*, and as the service ended, Dean's body was borne from the church. Five young men with whom he had played basketball in high school served as pallbearers.

The first chill of autumn in the Indiana air, James Byron Dean was buried beside his mother in a small cemetery at the edge of a cornfield, a patch of land, shaded by evergreens, that had once been an Indian burial ground.

# Debts and Acknowledgments

Much of the material in this book is based on personal reminiscences, and I would like to thank the following people who talked about Dean or wrote letters, and in some cases did both. Eddie Albert, Jean Alexander, the late Joseph Anthony, Margaret Barker, the late Barbara Baxley, James Bellah, Dr. Joseph B. Birdsell, Dr. Walden P. Boyle, Lew Bracker, the late Rogers Brackett, Frank Burns, Lon Chapman, David Clarke, Jeff Corey, Frank Corsaro, Sanger Crumpaker, Marion Daugherty, Ann Doran, Jeanette Miller Doty, the late Mildred Dunnock, Abe Feder, Paul Fix, the late Constance Ford, Ed Garrabrabt, the late Henry Ginsberg, Ruth Goetz, Manuel Gonzalez, the late Michael Gordon, Richard Grayson, Sir Alec Guinness, Pat Hardy, the late Tom Harmon, Matt Harlib, Robert Heller, Michael Higgins, George Roy Hill, Pat Hingle, the late John Houseman, the late Gusti Huber, Paul Huber, the late Christopher Isherwood, Anne Jackson, Billy James, Edgar Kahn, John Kalin, Lili Kardell, Elia Kazan, Bruce Kessler, Archer King, Piper Laurie, Ralph Levy, Jerry Lucce, Salem Ludwig, Sidney Lumet, the late John Lund, the late Daniel Mann, Arlene Sax Martell, the late Sal Mineo, Terry Moore, Ann McCormack, the late Clyde McCullough, Adeline Nall, Ralph Nelson, William F. Nolan, Jean N. Owen, Betsy Palmer, Arthur Penn, Nehemiah Persoff, Dan Petrie, John Peyser, Arthur Pierson, Barry Primus, Doris Quinlan, Ronald Reagan, Nicolas and Charlotte Romanos, Walter Ross, the late Mira Rostova, the late Beulah Roth, Howard Sackler, Sol Sacks, Roy

Schatt, the late Dore Schary, William Self, James Sheldon, Elizabeth Sheridan, Irving Shulman, the late Herman Shumlin, the late Robert Simon, the late Sidney Skolsky, Rusty Slocum, the late Leonard Spiegelgass, Bill Stevens, John Stix, Dennis Stock, Ernie Stockert, the late Lee Strasberg, Arnold Sundgaard, Florence Sundstrom, Lela Swift, Larry Swindell, Marc Towers, Eli Wallach, James Wasson, Ruth Waterbury, Paul Weaver, Christine White, the late Alec Wilder, and the late Ortense Winslow.

The following individuals provided background material, or helped with the project in other ways, checking facts, suggesting possible leads, in many instances taking time from their own busy schedules to lend their support: Ted Ashton, formerly of Warner Brothers publicity department (Ashton's press releases on Dean included many of the famous quotes which were picked up by Hollywood columnists and fan magazines, e.g., "I'm a serious-minded and intense little devil..." Perhaps more than any other person, he helped create the Dean legend.); Jay Barney; Julie Baumgold; John Behrens of CBS; Connie Berman and Bernadette Carrozza of Macfadden-Bartell Publications; Betty Ann Besch; Sylvia Bongiovanni of We Remember Dean International; Fred Coe; William Collins of the *Philadelphia Inquirer;* Earl Conrad; C. Ray Cooper, registrar of Santa Monica Junior College; Norman Corwin; Robert J. Costomiris; Pascal Covici, Jr.; John Crowell, researcher at the California State Library (Sacramento); Peggy Cummings, of the UCLA Alumni and Development Center; the late Jackie Curtis, formerly of Andy Warhol's Factory; Helen DeLuise; Digby Diehl, formerly of the *Los Angeles Times;* Richard H. Dodge, publications adviser, Santa Monica Junior College; Geraldine Duclow of the Philadelphia Free Library Theater Collection; George Eells; the late Morris L. Ernst, Esq.; Jack Garfein of the Actor and Director's Lab (Los Angeles); Elmer Gertz, Esq. (who kindly supplied me with Dean clippings over the years); Professor Vagn K. Hansen; Chandler Harris, public information manager (UCLA); Don

Herbert; Barbara Hillman of the *Dallas Morning News;* Val Holley; Lee Israel; Stephen Hanson and Stuart Ng, Warner Bros. Collection (USC); Hillary James and Bill Latham of Warner Brothers; Harry L. Lichtenbaum; Chris Kager of the New York Mets; Phil Lyman of the Gotham Book Mart; Mrs. Emma Mallan, former owner of the Paisano Hotel, Marfa, Texas; Gloria Mariano, formerly of Time, Inc.; the late Armina Marshall of the Theater Guild; Charles Martyn of the *Philadelphia Evening Bulletin;* Jerry Mastoli; Jim Matthews, historian of the California Sports Car club (which Dean had joined in early 1955); Worthington Miner and J. P. Nickel, formerly of Studio One; the late Dr. Paul Meyers and the staff of the Theater Collection of the New York Public Library; Mrs. Ann McCallum of the Marfa, Texas, Chamber of Commerce; Barry McCarthy; Norma Nannini of *Variety;* Vivian Nathan; Terry Ork; Marty Pitts; Martin Quigley, Jr.; Bonnie Rothbart of the library of the Academy of Motion Picture Arts and Sciences (Los Angeles); Andrew Sarris; Eileen Shanahan; Michael Sheridan; Charles Silver of the Museum of Modern Art Film History (New York); Elaine Steinbeck; Selma Tembler; Howard Thompson, formerly of the *New York Times;* Lou Valentino of Time, Inc.; Jerry Vermilye of *TV Guide;* Frank Wetzel of the New York Alumni Chapter of Sigma Nu Fraternity; Martha Wright of the Indiana State Library (Indianapolis).

I would also like to thank Robert Chuter of Australia for making available to me numerous items in his vast collection of James Dean memorabilia. David Garfield gave me access to his excellent work *(A Player's Place)* on the Actors Studio and helped me track down Dean's work there, which I might have otherwise overlooked. I am indebted to Carl Himmel for translating Kurt Kuberzig's *Von Film Fur Fans* (1962). Beverly Linet kindly shared with me her own store of knowledge from being a Hollywood correspondent in the 1950s. Leslie Aquaviva (now Shulman) aided me with my research in Los Angeles.

Two friends, William Bostock and Robert Hubbard, read the book in manuscript and made a number of valuable suggestions. I would like to thank Nora Ammar, Jamie Pitts, Vera Koulian, and Christina Coffelt for typing the manuscript and George Cuza for helping to retrace the route Jimmy took that fateful September day.

I also want to express my gratitude to my agent Roz Targ and my editor Allan J. Wilson for making this revised edition a reality.

# Bibliography

## Articles

Breen, Ed. "James Dean's Indiana." *Traces* (Fall 1989).

Henderickson, Paul. "Remembering James Dean Back Home in Indiana." *Los Angeles Times* (July 22, 1973).

Meltsir, Aljean. "James Dean—His Life and Loves." *Motion Picture* (September 1956).

Owen, Gene Nelson. "The Man Who Would Be Fifty: A Memory of James Dean." *Los Angeles Times* (February 8, 1991).

Raskin, Lee. "The Lost Porsche." *We Remember Dean International* (April–May 1992).

Ray, Nicholas. "Story Into Script." *Sight & Sound* (Autumn 1956).

Roth, Sanford H. "The Assignment I'll Never Forget: Jimmy Dean." *Popular Photography* (July 1962).

## Books

Adams, Leith, and Keith Burns. *Behind the Scene.* New York: Birch Lane Press, 1990.

Allan, James B. *Elizabeth Taylor.* Derby, Conn.: Monarch Books, 1962.

Backus, Jim. *Rocks on the Roof.* New York: G. P. Putnam's Sons, 1958.

Baker, Carroll. *Baby Doll.* New York: Arbor House, 1983.

Bast, William. *James Dean.* New York: Ballantine Books, 1958.

Beath, Warren Newton. *The Death of James Dean*. New York: Grove Press, 1986.

Beaton, Cecil. *Cecil Beaton's Fair Lady*. New York: Holt, 1964.

Conrad, Barnaby. *Matador*. Boston: Houghton Mifflin, 1961.

Conrad, Earl. *Billy Rose: Manhattan Primitive*. Cleveland: World Publishing, 1968.

Dalton, David, ed. *James Dean Revealed*. New York: Delta Books, 1991.

Dos Passos, John. *Midcentury*. Boston: Houghton Mifflin, 1961.

Ellis, Royston. *Rebel*. London: Consul Books, 1962.

Ferber, Edna. *A Kind of Magic*. Garden City: Doubleday, 1963.

Goodman, Ezra. *The Fifty-Year Decline and Fall of Hollywood*. New York: Simon & Schuster, 1961.

Gottlieb, Polly Rose. *The Nine Lives of Billy Rose*. New York: Crown, 1968.

Headrick, Robert Jr. *Deanmania: The Man, the Character, the Legend*. Las Vegas: Pioneer Books, 1990.

Hess, Alan. *Googie's: Fifties Coffee Shop Architecture*. San Francisco: Chronicle Books, 1986.

Holley, Val. *James Dean: Tribute to a Rebel*. Lincolnwood, Ill.: Publications International, 1991.

Hopper, Hedda (with James Brough). *The Whole Truth and Nothing But*. Garden City: Doubleday, 1963.

Hyams, Joe. *Mislaid in Hollywood*. New York: Peter H. Wyden, 1973.

Kael, Pauline. *I Lost It at the Movies*. Boston: Little, Brown, 1965.

Kazan, Elia. *A Life*. New York: Doubleday Anchor, 1989.

Morella, Joe, and Edward Z. Epstein. *Brando: The Unauthorized Biography*. New York: Crown, 1973.

Morin, Edgar. *The Stars*. New York: Grove Press, 1960.

Rees, Robert. *One Fan's Journey*. Katy, Tex.: Empire, Inc., 1995.

Riese, Randall. *James Dean: His Life and Legacy From A to Z*. Chicago: Contemporary Books, 1991.

Rivkin, Allen, and Laura Kerra, eds. *Hello, Hollywood!* Garden City: Doubleday, 1962.

Ross, Walter. *The Immortal*. New York: Simon & Schuster, 1958.

Saint Exupéry, Antoine de. *The Little Prince*. New York: Harcourt, Brace, and World, 1943.

Salgues, Yves. *James Dean: ou le mal de vivre*. Paris: Pierre Horay, 1957.

Sarris, Andrew. *Interviews With Film Directors*. Indianapolis: Bobbs-Merrill, 1968.

Schatt, Roy. *James Dean: A Portrait*. New York: Beaufort Books, 1982.

Stock, Dennis. *James Dean Revisited*. San Francisco: Chronicle Books, 1987.

Tanner, Louise. *Here Today*. New York: Thomas Y. Crowell, 1959.

Taylor, Elizabeth. *Elizabeth Taylor: An Informal Memoir*. New York, Harper & Row. 1965.

Thomas, T. T. *I, James Dean*. New York: Popular Library, 1957.

Van Doren, Mamie (with Art Aveilhe). *Playing the Field*. New York: Berkley Books, 1988.

# Index

# Index

# About the Author

RONALD MARTINETTI is a former book columnist for *Newsday*, the Long Island newspaper. Before that, he wrote for the *Wall Street Journal* where an editor described him as being "argumentative, temperamental, and not a good bet for future employment." After leaving journalism, he studied law at the University of Chicago Law School and is now a trial lawyer in Glendale, California.

When *The James Dean Story* was originally published in 1975, the book was called by the *Los Angeles Times* "the best and most objective account of Dean's life," and was translated into French, Japanese, and German.